UNDERSTANDING THE GODHEAD

GREGORY K. RIGGEN

Other Books by This Author:

Understanding the New Birth

Understanding Separation

Calling on the Name of the Lord (an in-home Bible Study)

Do All Speak with Tongues? (an in-home Bible Study)

Lessons on Prayer (download only)

Bible Reading Made Easy (daily reading chart; free download)

Order from:

The Truth Church of Olathe, Kansas

http://www.olathetruth.com/resources

All Scripture quotations are from the King James Version of the Holy Bible, unless otherwise noted.

Copyright © 2019 Gregory K. Riggen

All rights reserved.

ISBN-13: 978-1-7330572-0-2

DEDICATION

This book is dedicated to the One Who loved me enough to call me out of darkness into His marvelous light. I am forever grateful for the knowledge and understanding He has so graciously granted to me. He alone is God. He alone is worthy of praise. He alone has the name which is above all names, and that name is JESUS!

CONTENTS

	Acknowledgements	i
	Preface	1
	Introduction	7
1	God is One!	13
2	Identifying the Father	19
3	Identifying the Son	25
4	God in Christ	35
5	Providing Further Proof	49
6	Questions Answered	61
7	Conclusion	85

ACKNOWLEDGMENTS

I would like to express my sincere appreciation to everyone who helped make this book a reality. First, it was Bishop Gary Howard's encouragement that became the catalyst for me to write. Second, my wife has spent untold hours reading, re-reading, editing, and working alongside me throughout this process. Also, Brother Jared Hilton (my assistant) has gone above and beyond the call of duty in helping me with this effort. I also appreciate the others who served as proofreaders and editors, Brother John Burgess, Brother Mark Cowen, Brother James Short, and my son-in-law, Captain D.J. Uribe (USAF). Their input has been invaluable. Finally, I want to thank Sister Jasmine Olmos for the cover design. To each and every one of you, words are not adequate to convey my deep gratitude. The words, "Thank You!" just do not seem sufficient. Just know that I am truly thankful.

PREFACE
THE REASON FOR WRITING

For several years now, I have had people ask me to compile a book about Apostolic Doctrine. I have repeatedly shrugged off any such suggestions, as I recognize that (1) there are already many scholarly works available on every area of this truth, and (2) the way I teach doctrine is extremely simple and, accordingly, might be rejected by those expecting a more "scholarly" approach.

Several things happened that obviously brought about a change of mind. First was the tremendous success we have been seeing in converting Trinitarian preachers on the continent of Africa. This volume would be extremely lengthy if I described in detail just how successful we have been, so I will give just a brief synopsis.

Beginning in 2013, and continuing up until (and most likely long after) the printing of this book, God has enabled me to travel to a number of African countries and teach Apostolic Doctrine to literally hundreds of Trinitarian ministers and their wives. We have seen God repeatedly open their eyes to subjects such as the oneness of God, baptism in Jesus' name, the necessity of the Holy Ghost, and separation from the world. They, in turn, go back to their congregations and teach what they have learned. As a result, they have baptized the majority (if not all) of the members of their

The Reason for Writing

congregations. We give all the glory to God, as we recognize that this is a work of His Spirit, and not the results of our talents, abilities, or intellect. However, we also recognize that God has repeatedly used our simple, methodical presentation to accommodate this great revival.

The second thing that happened was I that suddenly received several invitations to teach doctrine in Apostolic churches here in the United States of America. Whenever I have accepted the invitation, I have made it a point to tell the host pastor and congregation that they should not expect any profundities, as I do not try to "go deep" in teaching these truths. Rather, I try to make our message as simple as possible, thereby making it understandable to virtually anyone with an open mind. What I have seen during these sessions has, quite honestly, amazed me. Over and over, good saints of God (some of whom have been, by their own testimony, "serving the Lord for many years") have come to me to thank me for helping them to get a better grasp of the truth and, in some cases, a revelation of truth for the very first time!

With these two factors already working together, the third and final factor came into play. While teaching at Tulsa Lighthouse Church in Tulsa, Oklahoma, the man I am privileged to call my pastor, Elder Gary Howard, asked me to write a book about our doctrine. My love and appreciation for Bishop Howard is deep. Any suggestions or requests that come from him carry much more weight with me than those of others. I knew when he brought it up that it was definitely time, and, within days, I sat down to begin this project.

As I worked, though, I soon felt overwhelmed with the task at hand. My original goal seemed daunting: I wanted to write one book that would cover three major doctrinal areas (the Godhead, the New Birth, and Separation). Because each of these subjects were so monumental in their scope, I simply could not seem to get motivated enough to "stay the course."

Eventually, a thought occurred to me. I decided that I should break each of these three subjects into books of their own. Doing so would condense the subject matter into "bite-sized pieces," allowing me to feel more like the task was doable.

What you hold in your hands is the first of what I expect to be at least three volumes, each focused on helping the reader to gain the proper understanding of a particular aspect of the Apostolic message. It is my hope that the subsequent volumes will come together quickly.

My intention and purpose for writing is to provide publications almost anyone can easily understand. I believe that there is a genuine need to present our message in a way that remains true to "the simplicity that is in Christ" (2 Corinthians 11:3). In fact, I believe that there is a real need in our movement to produce writings which can convince doubters and strengthen believers regardless of their spiritual or educational level.

Throughout the pages of this book, therefore, I hope to present the doctrine of the Godhead in such a way that "the wayfaring men, though fools, shall not err therein" (Isaiah 35:8). While I desire to be thorough, I have no intention of delving into a deep theological exegesis. Rather, I want to let Scripture interpret Scripture and thereby offer answers for the "common man."

This book is written in a conversational manner, as opposed to a more formal writing style. While some may prefer the latter, I am intentionally avoiding that approach. My goal is to present these truths in such a way that the reader can feel we are having a personal discussion, and not just being lectured.

Before beginning the studies at hand, I should take some time to provide a glimpse into my personal testimony. I was not born into an Apostolic home. While my parents considered themselves Christians, they were not "practicing" any particular religion.

The Reason for Writing

They instilled in us a belief in God, but that was about as far as it went. They did not teach us about the Bible, and they did not take us to church.

Through a series of events, God brought my family to a place of desperation. We went from having a comfortable income to extreme poverty in a matter of months. At the age of 11, a teenage cousin invited me to visit an Apostolic church. I went and loved it. We lived close enough that I could walk to church if necessary, and, shortly after turning 12, I was baptized in Jesus' name and filled with the Holy Ghost. That summer, I felt God's call to preach. Within a few months of my conversion, my parents, siblings, and grandmother were subsequently converted. About a year and a half after I prayed through, I preached my first sermon at the age of 13.

Not long after that, I was invited to attend a debate between an Apostolic preacher and a preacher from another denomination. I watched as the Apostolic preacher quoted Scriptures and defended the message, doing it all without hesitation. Something gripped my heart, and I was overcome with the feeling that "if he can know our doctrine that well, so can I." After attending several of these debates, I began my quest for doctrinal knowledge and understanding.

By the age of 14, I had compiled eight typed pages explaining why we baptize in Jesus' name. Three years later, during the summer between my junior and senior years in high school, I was invited to be the guest on a Christian radio talk show in Dallas, Texas, debating the subject of baptism. Within 10 years of that, God helped me to convert a Trinitarian pastor, baptizing his entire family and a number of his former members! Now, all these years later, the Lord has blessed me to be a part of a revival of Biblical proportions where hundreds upon hundreds are coming to the knowledge of the truth!

I only relate these things for the purpose of showing how

Apostolic doctrine has been the focal point of my life and ministry for many years. I am quite certain there are those who will find what I write to be elementary, and I am fine with that. I do not claim to be producing a doctoral thesis filled with profundities twice profounded. I am just a man with a strong passion for the truth who wants to help others comprehend it, accept it, believe it, obey it, and, most of all, love it!

There is a difference between knowledge and understanding. A person can have knowledge of certain facts, but not necessarily understand the meaning of those facts. For example, many high school graduates possess the knowledge that $E=mc^2$. Nevertheless, many of those same graduates have no understanding of what those symbols actually mean.

I hope the contents of this book will do more than simply provide you with a knowledge of the subject at hand. I hope it will also give you a very thorough understanding.

It is my sincere prayer that God will use this relatively short book for His glory, and that many will receive a revelation of truth as a result of having read it. If even one person is convinced, convicted, or converted, it will have been worth my time and effort.

The Reason for Writing

INTRODUCTION
DEFINING THE GODHEAD

Matthew 16:13-18

> *When Jesus came into the coasts of Caesarea Philippi, he asked his disciples, saying, Whom do men say that I the Son of man am?* [14]*And they said, Some say that thou art John the Baptist: some, Elias; and others, Jeremias, or one of the prophets.* [15]*He saith unto them, But whom say ye that I am?* [16]*And Simon Peter answered and said, Thou art the Christ, the Son of the living God.* [17]*And Jesus answered and said unto him, Blessed art thou, Simon Barjona: for flesh and blood hath not revealed it unto thee, but my Father which is in heaven.* [18]*And I say also unto thee, That thou art Peter, and upon this rock I will build my church; and the gates of hell shall not prevail against it.*

In the above text, Jesus first asked His disciples about the opinions of others concerning Who He was. The disciples responded with the things they had obviously heard. Next, Jesus asked a question that was far more important than the opinion of others—He wanted to know the opinion of His followers themselves. It was at that moment Peter made his well-known declaration.

Matthew 16:16
> *And Simon Peter answered and said, Thou art the Christ, the Son of the living God.*

There are a couple of things about this conversation which deserve our attention. First, according to Jesus, this understanding came by revelation from the Father.

Matthew 16:17
> *And Jesus answered and said unto him, Blessed art thou, Simon Barjona: for flesh and blood hath not revealed it unto thee, but my Father which is in heaven.*

Second, we must realize that this revelation is the foundation of the church. It is not an optional philosophy!

Matthew 16:18
> *And I say also unto thee, That thou art Peter, and upon this rock I will build my church; and the gates of hell shall not prevail against it.*

Understand that the church was not built on Peter. While his name in the original Greek certainly means a rock, the word is more specific. The Greek word petros actually signifies a small pebble. When Jesus said He would build His church on "this rock," He used a DIFFERENT Greek word. Here, He used petra, which signifies a large boulder! The rock upon which the church is built is the rock of the revelation of Who Christ is!

When writing to Timothy, Paul's "son in the gospel" (Philippians 2:19-22), the apostle made an interesting statement. Let us consider what he wrote.

1 Timothy 3:16
> *And without controversy great is the mystery of godliness: God was manifest in the flesh, justified in the Spirit, seen of angels, preached unto the Gentiles, believed on in the world, received up into glory.*

"Without controversy" is actually one word in the original Greek, and it means "by the consent of all." By context, it speaks of that which is agreed upon by all true believers.

The Greek word which is translated "godliness" is not the same word which is usually used to convey the concept of "godliness." Rather, it is a totally different word with a more far-reaching definition. According to Philip Schaff's *Popular Commentary on the New Testament,* "the word 'godliness' is taken [to mean] the religion which men profess."[1]

Often in my teaching I provide clear definitions of particular Greek words and phrases and then summarize them. When I do, I refer to the summary as "the *Riggen Revised Version" (RRV)*. The RRV of 1 Timothy 3:16 would read, "By the consent of all true believers, the basis of the Christian religion is the fact that God was manifest in the flesh."

We see, then, that Paul stated every true believer holds the same opinion concerning God. In Matthew 16:18, Jesus stated that the only church against which Hell cannot prevail is the church that is built upon the revelation of Who He is! Because of this fact, the Biblical doctrine of the Godhead is NOT something that can be left to personal opinions and private interpretations.

As we begin our pursuit of Scriptural understanding concerning the Godhead, let us do as Jesus did and find out the opinions that are commonly held. I feel confident in saying that the majority of theologians and scholars who identify themselves as Christian would define God as "the Holy Trinity."

The Trinity is commonly defined as: Three separate and distinct Persons Who are co-equal, co-eternal, and co-existent. To ensure I explain the Trinity in a manner acceptable to those espousing that doctrine, I searched for an accurate definition.

---

[1] SCHAFF, P. (1883). *A Popular Commentary on the New Testament.* Edinburgh, T. & T. Clark.

Defining the Godhead

The Alpha and Omega Ministries website identifies itself as being about "Christian apologetics" and "Theology."[2] There, the Trinity is defined as follows:

> 1. There is in the Divine Being but one indivisible essence (ousia, essentia).
>
> 2. In this one Divine Being there are three Persons or individual subsistences, Father, Son and Holy Spirit.
>
> 3. The whole undivided essence of God belongs equally to each of the three persons.
>
> 4. The subsistence and operation of the three persons in the divine Being is marked by a certain definite order.
>
> 5. There are certain personal attributes by which the three persons are distinguished.
>
> 6. The Church confesses the Trinity to be a mystery beyond the comprehension of man.[3]

Another website which seeks to address the doctrine of the Trinity is LayEvangelism.com. There, the following commentary is offered:

> Christian theologians have said "Deny the Trinity and you will lose your soul; try to explain it and you will lose your mind." ... God says in His word in Deuteronomy 29:29 "The secret things belong to Yehovah-our-Elohim..." There are some things about God we cannot understand on this side of heaven. As this verse states there are secrets that God shares with no one.

---

[2] Alpha and Omega Ministries, accessed April 29, 2019, https://www.aomin.org
[3] WHITE, J., *The Nature of God.* (2001). Alpha & Omega Ministries, http://vintage.aomin.org/natureofgod.html

> *The mystery of the Trinity is one of them. The Bible teaches us plainly that there is only one God of one essence from eternity past who is manifested in 3 individual persons who have independent intellect, emotion and will. This means that while these three persons who make up the ONE God are infinite God with all of the attributes of deity, yet their individual experiences and choices are unique. This does not mean that these are three individual God's [sic], this means that the ONE God of one essence is manifested in three individual persons.4*

The reason men teach that the Godhead is a "mystery beyond comprehension" is because THEIR definition of God IS beyond comprehension! In fact, the Apostle Paul stated the exact opposite. According to him, the Biblical definition of the Godhead is well within the grasp of human understanding.

Romans 1:20
For the invisible things of him from the creation of the world are clearly seen, being understood by the things that are made, even his eternal power and Godhead; so that they are without excuse:

Here Paul states that some things are "clearly seen" and "understood." Furthermore, those who fail to "clearly see" and "understand" them are "without excuse!" Interestingly, the apostle listed the Godhead among those things. Thus, not only CAN you understand it, and SHOULD you understand it, but you have no excuse for NOT understanding it!

Inasmuch as the Godhead can – and SHOULD – be understood, AND is NOT a "complex mystery," I contend that the

---

[4] KRUSE, D. P., *How Is One God of One Essence Manifested in Three Persons?*, (2004). Lay Evangelism,
http://www.layevangelism.com/qreference/islam/trinity.htm

Defining the Godhead

subject of the Godhead is actually one of profound simplicity. In the following chapters, we will examine four Scriptural principles that form the framework for all that is needed to understand the Godhead.

If a person can fully grasp (and accept) these four simple principles I provide in the following chapters, they will come to the conclusion that the Godhead truly IS a subject which is easy to comprehend. Furthermore, they will arrive at a proper Biblical interpretation of exactly Who the God of the Bible really is!

CHAPTER 1
GOD IS ONE!

The first principle that is key to understanding the Godhead is something upon which EVERY Christian should agree. It is: **There is only ONE GOD.**

> *Deuteronomy 6:4-5*
> *Hear, O Israel: The LORD our God is one LORD: ^{5}And thou shalt love the LORD thy God with all thine heart, and with all thy soul, and with all thy might.*

I believe it is necessary to emphasize the fact that to the Jewish people, this was the most important passage in the Scriptures. They made it a habit to repeat it every morning, every evening, and throughout the day; it was on a scroll that was nailed to the entryway of their homes.

Jesus even identified it as "the first of all commandments." (Many other translations, by the way, say Jesus called it "the most important.")

> *Mark 12:28-30*
> *And one of the scribes came, and having heard them reasoning together, and perceiving that he had answered them well, asked him, Which is the first commandment of all? ^{29}And Jesus answered*

God is One!

> him, *The first of all the commandments is, Hear, O Israel; The Lord our God is one Lord:* [30]*And thou shalt love the Lord thy God with all thy heart, and with all thy soul, and with all thy mind, and with all thy strength: this is the first commandment.*

In this passage, the scribe asked Jesus, "which is the first commandment of all?" With more than 600 commandments in the Old Testament, some might see that question as being difficult to answer. In spite of that fact, Jesus had no problem responding. He clearly stated that the most important commandment in the Bible was found in Deuteronomy 6:4-5!

It is important when reading Deuteronomy 6:4-5 that you notice verses four and five are one continual sentence. Although they are divided into two verses, it is a singular statement, and should be read as such. The reason I point this out is because of the slight difference between the way Matthew and Mark recorded Jesus' response.

While Matthew only quoted the latter portion—"thou shalt love the Lord thy God…" (see Matthew 22:36-38)—we should note that he was writing to a Jewish audience. The Jews, of course, would have readily recognized this as part of the one sentence found in Deuteronomy 6:4-5. Therefore, they would have immediately known that the first portion of that sentence ("Hear, O, Israel…") was obviously a part of the "first commandment" of which Jesus spoke.

Mark, on the other hand, wrote to a Roman audience—people who believed in more than one god. For them, it was necessary to include the entire sentence.

Considering this, it can be easily said that BOTH the knowledge of God's oneness AND the requirement of loving Him wholeheartedly make up the ONE "great commandment." The fact is, it does no good to simply know there is one God if you do

14

not love Him with all your heart, soul, mind, and strength. Furthermore, it does no good to love just any "god"—it MUST be the One True God of the Old Testament!

From this perspective, it is clear that the first and greatest commandment includes the fact that God is one. Thus, WHATEVER we believe about God, it MUST be built on the principle that He is ONE. Period.

There are far too many verses in the Bible which proclaim that God is one for me to provide an exhaustive list in this chapter. Nevertheless, I will provide several so that the reader can see how adamant the Scripture is that there is only one Lord.

> *Deuteronomy 4:35*
> *Unto thee it was shewed, that thou mightest know that the LORD he is God; there is none else beside him.*
>
> *Deuteronomy 4:39*
> *Know therefore this day, and consider it in thine heart, that the LORD he is God in heaven above, and upon the earth beneath: there is none else.*
>
> *Deuteronomy 32:39*
> *See now that I, even I, am he, and there is no god with me: I kill, and I make alive; I wound, and I heal: neither is there any that can deliver out of my hand.*
>
> *2 Samuel 7:22*
> *Wherefore thou art great, O LORD God: for there is none like thee, neither is there any God beside thee, according to all that we have heard with our ears.*
>
> *1 Kings 8:60*
> *That all the people of the earth may know that the LORD is God, and that there is none else.*

2 Kings 5:15

And he returned to the man of God, he and all his company, and came, and stood before him: and he said, Behold, now I know that there is no God in all the earth, but in Israel: now therefore, I pray thee, take a blessing of thy servant.

1 Chronicles 17:20

O LORD, there is none like thee, neither is there any God beside thee, according to all that we have heard with our ears.

Nehemiah 9:6

Thou, even thou, art LORD alone; thou hast made heaven, the heaven of heavens, with all their host, the earth, and all things that are therein, the seas, and all that is therein, and thou preservest them all; and the host of heaven worshippeth thee.

Psalms 86:10

For thou art great, and doest wondrous things: thou art God alone.

Isaiah 37:16

O LORD of hosts, God of Israel, that dwellest between the cherubims, thou art the God, even thou alone, of all the kingdoms of the earth: thou hast made heaven and earth.

Isaiah 43:10-11

Ye are my witnesses, saith the LORD, and my servant whom I have chosen: that ye may know and believe me, and understand that I am he: before me there was no God formed, neither shall there be after me. I I, even I, am the LORD; and beside me there is no saviour.

Isaiah 45:21

Tell ye, and bring them near; yea, let them take counsel together: who hath declared this from ancient time? who hath told it from that time? have not I the LORD? and there is no God else beside me; a just God and a Saviour; there is none beside me.

Isaiah 46:9

Remember the former things of old: for I am God, and there is none else; I am God, and there is none like me,

Malachi 2:10

Have we not all one father? hath not one God created us? why do we deal treacherously every man against his brother, by profaning the covenant of our fathers?

Mark 12:32

And the scribe said unto him, Well, Master, thou hast said the truth: for there is one God; and there is none other but he:

John 17:3

And this is life eternal, that they might know thee the only true God, and Jesus Christ, whom thou hast sent.

Romans 3:30

Seeing it is one God, which shall justify the circumcision by faith, and uncircumcision through faith.

1 Corinthians 8:4-6

As concerning therefore the eating of those things that are offered in sacrifice unto idols, we know that an idol is nothing in the world, and that there is none other God but one. 5For though there be that are called gods, whether in heaven or in earth, (as there be gods many, and lords many,) 6But to us there is but one God, the Father, of whom are all things, and we in him; and one Lord Jesus Christ, by whom are all things, and we by him.

Ephesians 4:6

One God and Father of all, who is above all, and through all, and in you all.

1 Timothy 2:5

For there is one God, and one mediator between God and men, the man Christ Jesus;

James 2:19

Thou believest that there is one God; thou doest well: the devils also believe, and tremble.

Thus, the most important concept is that God is ONE. This is the first principle in understanding the Godhead: **THERE IS ONLY ONE GOD.**

CHAPTER 2
IDENTIFYING THE FATHER

Although it should be obvious to all, it is worth stating that if ANYONE could identify Who God is, it would be Jesus Christ. Thus, HIS definition of God is far more important than ANY modern scholar or theologian. Let us, then, consider a conversation in which Jesus DID identify the proper way we should view God.

John 4:24
God is a Spirit: and they that worship him must worship him in spirit and in truth.

In this brief verse, we find the simple definition of exactly Who (and WHAT) God is. According to Jesus, the one God of the Bible is a Spirit. Please note that He NEVER said, "God is three persons," or even that "God is A person." Rather, He said, "God is a Spirit."

Accordingly, let us adopt the BIBLICAL identification of God – He is not three persons, two persons, or even ONE person. According to Jesus, God is a Spirit.

Based on that fact, consider the context of verse 24. In so doing, we see that Spirit we call "God" was identified by Christ as "the Father."

John 4:23-24

But the hour cometh, and now is, when the true worshippers shall worship the Father in spirit and in truth: for the Father seeketh such to worship him. ^{24}God is a Spirit: and they that worship him must worship him in spirit and in truth.

In verse 23, Jesus said the true worshippers would "worship the Father in spirit and in truth." He went on to say it is the Father Who is seeking "such to worship Him." In verse 24, the pronoun "him" refers to the antecedent "God." This verse goes on to say that "God" is the One Who must be worshipped "in spirit and truth." It is obvious from these two verses, then, that when Jesus spoke of "God," He was speaking of "the Father."

In fact, it is interesting to see how many times the New Testament specifically identifies "God" as "the Father" (for example, see John 6:27; John 8:41; Romans 1:7; Romans 15:6; 1 Corinthians 1:3; 1 Corinthians 8:6; 1 Corinthians 5:24; 2 Corinthians 1:2, 3; 2 Corinthians 11:31; Galatians 1:3, 4; Ephesians 1:2, 3, 17; Ephesians 6:23; Philippians 1:2; Philippians 2:11; Colossians 1:2; 1 Thessalonians 1:1; 1 Thessalonians 3:13; 2 Thessalonians 1:1, 2; 1 Timothy 1:2; 2 Timothy 1:2; Titus 1:4; Philemon 1:3; James 3:9; 1 Peter 1:2; 2 Peter 1:17; 2 John 1:3; Jude 1:1; *et al*).

Accordingly, it would be correct to render verse 24 as "God (the Father) is a Spirit." Therefore, any time we read about "the Father," we should immediately think "Spirit."

This fact irrefutably destroys the Trinitarian perception of Who the Father is. The Father cannot be "the first person in the Godhead," since He is not a "person" at all – He is a Spirit!

We all KNOW what the word "person" means! It clearly and undeniably refers to a human being (look it up in any dictionary if you doubt me on this), and – make no mistake – God is NOT a human being!

> **Numbers 23:19**
> *God is not a man, that he should lie; neither the son of man, that he should repent: hath he said, and shall he not do it? or hath he spoken, and shall he not make it good?*
>
> **1 Samuel 15:29**
> *And also the Strength of Israel will not lie nor repent: for he is not a man, that he should repent.*

To be fair, I have read where some Trinitarians today are starting to shy away from using the term "person" to describe God. The problem is that they would have to change their entire definition of the Godhead (i.e., "three persons") in order to quit using the term. So that they do not have to change their basic definition, they instead define "person" in a way that can fit their own ideology. One example is offered by the Christian Apologetics and Research Ministry (CARM), which defines "person" as "individuality and self-awareness."[5]

Perhaps I am being too simplistic, but it seems to me that if you have to come up with new definitions of common words in order to support your doctrine, you should immediately recognize that your doctrine is not correct! Regardless of the way in which Trinitarians want to define the word "person," the fact remains that God is far bigger, far more powerful, and far greater in every way than any "person" could ever be!

There are, of course, those who would insist that God IS, indeed, a "person," according to Scripture. Their claim is based on Hebrews 1:3.

> **Hebrews 1:3**
> *Who being the brightness of his glory, and the*

---

[5] SLICK, M., *What is the Trinity?*, (2008). Christian Apologetics and Research Ministry, https://carm.org/what-is-the-trinity

> *express image of his person, and upholding all things by the word of his power, when he had by himself purged our sins, sat down on the right hand of the Majesty on high;*

In this verse, the Bible says that Christ is the "express image of His [God the Father's] **person**." Although the King James Version translates the Greek word hupostasis as "person," it is virtually alone in doing so. Other translations render this word as "essence," "nature," or "being."

Concerning Hebrews 1:3, Dr. Albert Barnes said, "It is evident that it cannot be used in [the sense of a 'person'] when applied to God, and that this word ['person'] does not express the true idea of the passage here."[6] Obviously, the author of Hebrews was not trying to state that the Father is a "person," and Christ bears His "image," but rather that Christ is the full representation of the Father's essence and nature.

It goes without saying that we should accept the words of Jesus at face value rather than trying to interpolate them to fit our own beliefs. If we do so, we will have to admit that God the Father is a Spirit and NOT a person!

Understanding that God the Father is a Spirit, let us consider some very important attributes of that Spirit:

1. **God the Father is an Omnipresent Spirit** (*i.e.*, He is everywhere at the same time).

> ### *Isaiah 66:1*
> *Thus saith the LORD, The heaven is my throne, and the earth is my footstool: where is the house that ye build unto me? and where is the place of my rest?*

---

[6] BARNES, A., Murphy, J. G., Cook, F. C., Pusey, E. B., Leupold, H. C., & Frew, R., (1996). Barnes' Notes. Grand Rapids, Michigan: Baker.

Psalm 139:7-10

Whither shall I go from thy spirit? or whither shall I flee from thy presence? ⁸If I ascend up into heaven, thou art there: if I make my bed in hell, behold, thou art there. ⁹If I take the wings of the morning, and dwell in the uttermost parts of the sea; ¹⁰Even there shall thy hand lead me, and thy right hand shall hold me.

Jeremiah 23:24

Can any hide himself in secret places that I shall not see him? saith the LORD. Do not I fill heaven and earth? saith the LORD.

2. **God the Father is an Immortal Spirit** (*i.e.*, He is everlasting and cannot die).

Psalm 90:1-4

LORD, thou hast been our dwelling place in all generations. ²Before the mountains were brought forth, or ever thou hadst formed the earth and the world, even from everlasting to everlasting, thou art God. ³Thou turnest man to destruction; and sayest, Return, ye children of men. ⁴For a thousand years in thy sight are but as yesterday when it is past, and as a watch in the night.

1 Timothy 1:17

Now unto the King eternal, immortal, invisible, the only wise God, be honour and glory for ever and ever. Amen.

1 Timothy 6:16

Who only hath immortality, dwelling in the light which no man can approach unto; whom no man hath seen, nor can see: to whom be honour and power everlasting. Amen.

3. **God the Father is an Invisible Spirit** (*i.e.*, He cannot be seen).

> **John 1:18**
>
> *No man hath seen God at any time; the only begotten Son, which is in the bosom of the Father, he hath declared him.*
>
> **Colossians 1:15**
>
> *Who is the image of the invisible God, the firstborn of every creature:*
>
> **1 Timothy 1:17**
>
> *Now unto the King eternal, immortal, invisible, the only wise God, be honour and glory for ever and ever. Amen.*
>
> **1 John 4:12**
>
> *No man hath seen God at any time. If we love one another, God dwelleth in us, and his love is perfected in us.*
>
> **1 Timothy 6:16**
>
> *Who only hath immortality, dwelling in the light which no man can approach unto; whom no man hath seen, nor can see: to whom be honour and power everlasting. Amen.*

None of these aspects and characteristics of God the Father are applicable to a "person" (as we understand the term). Instead, they clearly identify Him in such a way that we should readily confess that He is not – nor can He be – a man.

This knowledge helps us further gain a Biblical understanding of Who God is. This is, then, the second principle in understanding the Godhead: **THE ONE GOD OF THE BIBLE (the Father) IS A SPIRIT.**

CHAPTER 3
IDENTIFYING THE SON

We have determined from Scriptures that: (1) there is only one God; and (2) the one God (the Father) is a Spirit. Let us now focus our attention on the One commonly called "the Second Person in the Godhead" – the man Christ Jesus. In so doing, we will discover the third principle in this process of understanding the Godhead.

In order to identify the Son of God, I call your attention to the words of the angel Gabriel. When making the announcement to Mary that she was going to give birth to the Messiah, Gabriel made an interesting statement regarding the child she would deliver.

> ***Luke 1:35***
> *And the angel answered and said unto her, The Holy Ghost shall come upon thee, and the power of the Highest shall overshadow thee: therefore also that holy thing which shall be born of thee shall be called the Son of God.*

Before we get to the statement concerning the Son, let me highlight something else the angel proclaimed at that time. The first thing to note is that Gabriel said it was the Holy Ghost which would perform the miracle of paternity upon the womb of Mary.

It is a biological fact that when a woman is impregnated, whoever causes that woman to be with child is the child's father.

Identifying the Son

By simple logic, then, it should be evident that the Father of Jesus Christ was the Holy Ghost!

Luke is not the only writer to state this fact. The Book of Matthew also confirms this.

Matthew 1:18
Now the birth of Jesus Christ was on this wise: When as his mother Mary was espoused to Joseph, before they came together, she was found with child of the Holy Ghost.

Matthew 1:20
But while he thought on these things, behold, the angel of the Lord appeared unto him in a dream, saying, Joseph, thou son of David, fear not to take unto thee Mary thy wife: for that which is conceived in her is of the Holy Ghost.

With that being the case, we are left with only a few options: either Jesus had more than one Father, OR Jesus was confused about Who His Father was, OR the Holy Ghost (or "Holy Spirit," which by virtue of the very name, is understood to be a Spirit) IS the Father! The only logical conclusion that can be drawn is the last one. It is impossible for the Father to be "the First Person" and the Holy Spirit to be the "Third Person," since the Holy Spirit actually "fathered" the Christ child! Inasmuch as the Father is a Spirit and the Holy Ghost is a Spirit, yet there is only "one Spirit," there can be no distinction in the identity of God the Father and the Holy Ghost.

Ephesians 4:4
There is one body, and one Spirit, even as ye are called in one hope of your calling;

Since God the Father is a Spirit (John 4:24) Who is repeatedly called "the Holy One" (see 2 Kings 19:22; Psalm 71:22; Psalm 78:41; Psalm 89:18; Isaiah 1:4; Isaiah 5:19, 24; Isaiah 10:17, 20; Isaiah 12:6; Isaiah 17:7; Isaiah 29:19, 23; Isaiah

30:11, 12, 15, 29; Isaiah 31:1; Isaiah 37:23; Isaiah 41:14, 16, 20; Isaiah 43:3, 14, 15; Isaiah 45:11; Isaiah 47:4; Isaiah 48:17; Isaiah 49:7; Isaiah 54:5; Isaiah 55:5; Isaiah 60:9, 14; Jeremiah 50:29; Jeremiah 51:5; Ezekiel 20:39; Ezekiel 39:7; *et al*), AND there is only "one Spirit" (Ephesians 4:4), then God the Father MUST BE the Holy Spirit. There can be no distinction between the substance of the Father and the Holy Ghost.

Of course, the question no doubt comes to the minds of many, "Why, then, do we read references to both 'the Father' AND the 'Holy Ghost'?" The answer is simple: These are titles which identify positions of relationship.

Let me explain. I am a pastor and a husband. While both titles apply to the same individual, the titles are not necessarily interchangeable at all times. When I preach, for example, I do not say to the church, "Your husband is preaching to you." Nor do I come home and say to my wife, "Your pastor would like something to drink." In either situation, I will identify myself by the title which most accurately describes my relationship with the hearers.

Furthermore, it might be appropriate under the proper circumstances to use both titles in one sentence. For instance, a member of the church I oversee may speak of the example I set in my life as a pastor and husband. The use of two separate terms to describe me should, of course, never be taken as a reference to two separate individuals.

This One God will be referred to as "Father" if the subject at hand is, for example, His relationship with His creation (especially His people). He will also be called "the Holy Spirit" if the writer is describing the indwelling (or empowering) Spirit Who works in the lives of His people. Still, the Scripture might also use both terms if there is a need to address both roles at the same time.

Psalms 51:10-11
Create in me a clean heart, O God; and renew

a right spirit within me. ¹¹*Cast me not away from thy presence; and take not thy holy spirit from me.*

In this passage, although David did not address God specifically as "Father," he was obviously appealing to Him in that manner. Then, in the next verse, the Psalmist implored his Heavenly Father to not take the "Holy Spirit" from him. This is clearly not a reference to two separate Beings; rather, it is a reference to two separate positions held by the same Being in the life of the author.

We see this same thing in the New Testament. In the following verse, the Apostle Peter used more than one title to describe the same Being.

1 Peter 1:2
Elect according to the foreknowledge of God the Father, through sanctification of the Spirit, unto obedience and sprinkling of the blood of Jesus Christ: Grace unto you, and peace, be multiplied.

Here, Peter spoke of the Father's foreknowledge. He also mentioned the fact that we are sanctified by the Spirit. These terms should not be misunderstood as representing "two separate and distinct persons," but rather two separate and distinct functions of the one true God. (See 1 John 5:20.)

Let us now turn our attention once again to the verse of Scripture with which we opened this chapter. It is at this point that we will see the third principle involved in understanding the Godhead.

Luke 1:35
And the angel answered and said unto her, The Holy Ghost shall come upon thee, and the power of the Highest shall overshadow thee: therefore also that holy thing which shall be born of thee shall be called the Son of God.

The second thing that should be noted in this verse is "that which was born of Mary" was what would be called "the Son of God." In order to better understand my point, I want to call your attention to something Jesus said to Nicodemus when discussing the subject of birth.

John 3:6
That which is born of the flesh is flesh; and that which is born of the Spirit is spirit.

Since Mary was flesh, she did NOT give birth to a spirit. As flesh, she could only give birth to flesh. Therefore, "that which was born of Mary" was flesh. Hence, the "holy thing" that was to be called "the Son of God" was flesh.

Nowhere in the Scripture was Christ ever called "God the Son." Rather, He was the Son of God. There is a difference!

Remember, God is a Spirit. Again, Mary did NOT give birth to a spirit.

According to the angel Gabriel, the Son of God was the fleshly body (or humanity) which was born to Mary. Furthermore, the angel was not the only one to say this. The Apostle Paul confirmed this fact when he wrote that the Son of God was "made of a woman."

Galatians 4:4
But when the fulness of the time was come, God sent forth his Son, made of a woman, made under the law,

Let me be clear: Mary was NOT "the mother of God." Rather, she was the mother of the Son of God!

The fact that the term "Son of God" refers to the humanity (the flesh) is evidenced by the following references to those things which accompany humanity, but do not describe spirits:

(1) He grew physically, intellectually, emotionally, and spiritually.

Identifying the Son

Luke 2:52

And Jesus increased in wisdom and stature, and in favour with God and man.

(2) He got hungry.

Matthew 4:2

And when he had fasted forty days and forty nights, he was afterward an hungred.

(3) He grew weary.

John 4:6

Now Jacob's well was there. Jesus therefore, being wearied with his journey, sat thus on the well: and it was about the sixth hour.

(4) He slept.

Matthew 8:24

And, behold, there arose a great tempest in the sea, insomuch that the ship was covered with the waves: but he was asleep.

(5) He wept.

John 11:35

Jesus wept.

(6) He called Himself "the Son of Man."

Matthew 16:13

When Jesus came into the coasts of Caesarea Philippi, he asked his disciples, saying, Whom do men say that I the Son of man am?

(7) He called Himself "a man."

John 8:40

But now ye seek to kill me, a man that hath told you the truth, which I have heard of God: this did not Abraham.

(8) He died.

> **John 19:33**
> But when they came to Jesus, and saw that he was dead already, they brake not his legs:

> **1 Corinthians 15:3**
> For I delivered unto you first of all that which I also received, how that Christ died for our sins according to the scriptures;

It is clear that a spirit does not get smarter, get hungry, or get weary. A spirit does not sleep nor weep. A spirit could never be "the son of man" or "a man." A spirit does not die. These references show beyond the shadow of a doubt that the Son of God was a man – fully human in every sense of the word. His flesh was not "divine flesh" (there is no such thing ever described in the Bible; in fact 1 Peter 1:24 says, "ALL flesh is as grass [which] withereth, and ... falleth away). His flesh was the same as His mother's.

It is indisputable that the term "Son of God" refers to the humanity of Christ. It deals with His flesh.

It should be pointed out here that, while we believe in the Eternal Father and, therefore, the Eternal Spirit, we do NOT believe in the Eternal Son. In fact, the Bible says the exact opposite.

> **John 3:16**
> For God so loved the world, that he gave his only begotten Son, that whosoever believeth in him should not perish, but have everlasting life.

In what may be one of the most well-known (and perhaps beloved) verses used by Trinitarians, the Son is said to be "begotten." "Begotten" and "eternal" are contradictory terms. "Begotten" means to have a beginning, but that which is eternal has no beginning. So to identify Christ as the "begotten" Son is the exact opposite of calling Him the "eternal Son."

The Book of Hebrews even states that there was a specific

day which marked the beginning of the Son of God.

Hebrews 1:5

For unto which of the angels said he at any time, Thou art my Son, this day have I begotten thee? And again, I will be to him a Father, and he shall be to me a Son?

Furthermore, the Bible speaks of the day in which the office of Son will cease to exist.

1 Corinthians 15:24-28

Then cometh the end, when he shall have delivered up the kingdom to God, even the Father; when he shall have put down all rule and all authority and power. ^{25}For he must reign, till he hath put all enemies under his feet. ^{26}The last enemy that shall be destroyed is death. ^{27}For he hath put all things under his feet. But when he saith, all things are put under him, it is manifest that he is excepted, which did put all things under him. ^{28}And when all things shall be subdued unto him, then shall the Son also himself be subject unto him that put all things under him, that God may be all in all.

If the Son had a specific day in which He was begotten (or had a beginning) AND will have a specific day in which He "delivers up" the kingdom (or ends His role), then, by definition, the Son is NOT "eternal." Again, the term "Son" refers to "that which was born of Mary" (according to Luke 1:35).

The purpose of the Son was redemption (completed at Calvary), mediation (on-going until the rapture), returning in glory, and reigning 1,000 years. When all of this is completed, God (the Spirit) will be "all in all."

In discussing the fact that the Son is NOT eternal, it is important to address the supposed references to the Son which appear in the Old Testament. If, as I have put forward, the Son did not exist at that time (at least not as the Son), then there must be a valid explanation for any Old Testament references which use the term.

Without question, there IS an explanation which is actually quite simple. Any passage that truly makes mention of the Son of God in the Old Testament was prophetic. Such is the case in the following verse from Proverbs.

> **Proverbs 30:4**
> Who hath ascended up into heaven, or descended? who hath gathered the wind in his fists? who hath bound the waters in a garment? who hath established all the ends of the earth? what is his name, and what is his son's name, if thou canst tell?

In order to properly interpret this verse, it is important to consider the context in which it was written. To do that, one must, of course, pay attention to the first verse of this chapter.

> **Proverbs 30:1**
> The words of Agur the son of Jakeh, even the prophecy: the man spake unto Ithiel, even unto Ithiel and Ucal,

The writer clearly identifies this passage as "the prophecy." He was not speaking of things that existed in the present tense. He was speaking prophetically of things that were to come.

Other Old Testament passages that seem to refer to the Son, but are not prophetic in nature, are generally misunderstood (at best), and perhaps even misconstrued. A close examination of these verses will show the serious student of Scripture that they do NOT, in fact, mention the Son as being in existence at that time.

One example of an oft-quoted (but misinterpreted) verse comes from the Book of Daniel. Here, the King James Bible quotes King Nebuchadnezzar as saying he saw the form of the fourth man in the fiery furnace as being "like the Son of God."

> **Daniel 3:25**
> He answered and said, Lo, I see four men loose, walking in the midst of the fire, and they have no hurt; and the form of the fourth is like the Son of God.

To properly understand this verse, remember who is speaking. Nebuchadnezzar was a heathen king who had no concept of "the Son of God" (as far as the way the term is used in the New Testament). It is unfortunate that any translation would read that way, especially since the actual Hebrew reads, "the form of the fourth is like a son of the gods!"

As a pagan, Nebuchadnezzar worshipped many false gods. What he saw that day resembled a man ("a son"), yet was obviously reflective of Divinity ("the gods").

In order for the Son of God (who was "made of a woman") to exist in the Old Testament (or before), the woman of whom He was "made" would have had to have existed at that time as well. Thus, a preexistent Son requires Him to have a preexistent mother!

As I conclude this chapter, let me remind you of something important. Based on the second principle we presented to help you understand the Godhead, when we read "Father," we should immediately think "Spirit" or Deity. In the same fashion, when we read "Son," we should immediately think "Flesh" or Humanity. This is, then, the third principle in understanding the Godhead: **THE SON WAS BORN OF A WOMAN AND WAS, THEREFORE, FLESH.**

CHAPTER 4
GOD IN CHRIST

If a person were to take the things I have written in Chapter 3 without continuing on into what I am about to discuss, they could easily arrive at an erroneous conclusion. They might decide that I am claiming that Jesus Christ was ONLY a man. However, that is FAR from the truth.

This chapter may well be the most important chapter in this book. Here, I intend to not only bring all three of the previously discussed principles together, but, with the addition of the fourth principle, offer a full and complete explanation of the Biblical view of the Godhead (including the true identity of Jesus Christ).

Let us go to Paul's second letter to the church at Corinth and find there a clear and concise statement which forms the basis of the Scriptural truth concerning the Godhead. As you read this verse, I ask you to apply a rule I gave in Chapter 2 as well as a rule given in Chapter 3. Those two rules are:

(1) When we read God (or "the Father"), we should immediately think "Spirit."

(2) When we read "Christ" (or "the Son"), we should immediately think "Flesh."

> **2 Corinthians 5:19**
>
> *To wit, that God was in Christ, reconciling the world unto himself, not imputing their trespasses unto them; and hath committed unto us the word of reconciliation.*

Applying the above-stated rules, we can rightfully interpret the verse (as I would in the *Riggen Revised Version*, should such a book exist): **"To wit that the Spirit was in the Flesh, reconciling the world unto HIMSELF."**

Rather than the Father being a separate "person" from the Son, Paul stated that the Father was IN the Son. Notice also that God and Christ were not reconciling the world to "themselves." He used the singular term "Himself" to describe the One Whose outward flesh (i.e., "the Son") was indwelt by the inward Spirit (i.e., "the Father"). Thus, the Godhead can be explained like this: the Eternal Spirit called the Father indwelt the begotten flesh known as the Son. The Spirit in the flesh obviously makes just one individual. That individual is the One we know as Jesus Christ!

As I said in my opening paragraph, it is erroneous to say that I believe Jesus was JUST a man. According to the Scriptures, Jesus was both God AND man. On the outside (His humanity), He was the Son. On the inside (His Deity), He was the Father!

The fact that Jesus was both God (the Father) and man (the Son) is evidenced by the following references which clearly describe what has been called His "dual nature:"

1. **He was a man.**

   > **John 8:40**
   >
   > *But now ye seek to kill me, a man that hath told you the truth, which I have heard of God: this did not Abraham.*

   a. Yet Thomas called Him "God."

John 20:28
And Thomas answered and said unto him, My Lord and my God.

2. **The Jews rightfully said He was not 50 years old.**

John 8:57
Then said the Jews unto him, Thou art not yet fifty years old, and hast thou seen Abraham?

   a. **Yet He existed before Abraham.**

John 8:58
Jesus said unto them, Verily, verily, I say unto you, Before Abraham was, I am.

3. **He increased in wisdom.**

Luke 2:52
And Jesus increased in wisdom and stature, and in favour with God and man.

   a. **Yet Peter said Jesus knew "all things."**

John 21:17
He saith unto him the third time, Simon, son of Jonas, lovest thou me? Peter was grieved because he said unto him the third time, Lovest thou me? And he said unto him, Lord, thou knowest all things; thou knowest that I love thee. Jesus saith unto him, Feed my sheep.

4. **He is described in various passages as being weak and weary.**

2 Corinthians 13:4
For though he was crucified through weakness, yet he liveth by the power of God. For we also are weak in him, but we shall live with him by the power of God toward you.

John 4:6
Now Jacob's well was there. Jesus therefore,

being wearied with his journey, sat thus on the well: and it was about the sixth hour.

    a.   **Yet He described Himself as the Almighty.**

Revelation 1:8

I am Alpha and Omega, the beginning and the ending, saith the Lord, which is, and which was, and which is to come, the Almighty.

5.   **He was on earth.**

Matthew 9:6

But that ye may know that the Son of man hath power on earth to forgive sins, (then saith he to the sick of the palsy,) Arise, take up thy bed, and go unto thine house.

    a.   **Yet He said He was in Heaven.**

John 3:13

And no man hath ascended up to heaven, but he that came down from heaven, even the Son of man which is in heaven.

6.   **He prayed.**

Luke 22:41

And he was withdrawn from them about a stone's cast, and kneeled down, and prayed,

    a.   **Yet He is the One Who answers prayer.**

John 14:14

If ye shall ask any thing in my name, I will do it.

You should not see two separate persons in these scriptures. Rather, you should see one Person Who has two natures! Because of that, at any given time He could act and speak from either of two very different standpoints: He could act and speak as a man, or He could act and speak as God.

Understanding the Godhead

When reading about events and statements in the life of Jesus, you need only ask yourself, "In this passage, is He acting as God or acting as man? Is He speaking as God or speaking as man?" Understanding this apparent dichotomy is actually quite easy when viewed through the lens of His dual nature, as the following examples should prove:

1. **When Jesus said the flesh is weak, He spoke as a man.**

Matthew 26:41
Watch and pray, that ye enter not into temptation: the spirit indeed is willing, but the flesh is weak.

    a. **When He said all power was His, He spoke as God.**

Matthew 28:18
And Jesus came and spake unto them, saying, All power is given unto me in heaven and in earth.

2. **When He rode the ship across the sea, He acted as a man.**

Matthew 14:13
When Jesus heard of it, he departed thence by ship into a desert place apart: and when the people had heard thereof, they followed him on foot out of the cities.

    a. **When He walked on the water, He acted as God.**

Matthew 14:25
And in the fourth watch of the night Jesus went unto them, walking on the sea.

Job 9:8
Which alone spreadeth out the heavens, and treadeth upon the waves of the sea.

3. **When He said, "I thirst," He spoke as a man.**

John 19:28

After this, Jesus knowing that all things were now accomplished, that the scripture might be fulfilled, saith, I thirst.

a. When He said, "If any man thirst, let him come to me and drink," He spoke as God.

John 7:37

In the last day, that great day of the feast, Jesus stood and cried, saying, If any man thirst, let him come unto me, and drink.

4. When He asked for help in the garden, He acted as a man.

Matthew 26:39

And he went a little further, and fell on his face, and prayed, saying, O my Father, if it be possible, let this cup pass from me: nevertheless not as I will, but as thou wilt.

a. When He miraculously helped others, He acted as God.

Matthew 15:25

Then came she and worshipped him, saying, Lord, help me.

Matthew 15:28

Then Jesus answered and said unto her, O woman, great is thy faith: be it unto thee even as thou wilt. And her daughter was made whole from that very hour.

While even some Trinitarians will agree that Jesus had a dual nature, and perhaps even go so far as to admit He was both God and man, they often stop short of a very important truth. Because He was both God (the Spirit) and man (the flesh), He was both Father and Son!

I realize that there are many who will take issue with this last statement. Nevertheless, I can state unequivocally that anyone who cannot accept that Jesus could be both Father and Son at the same time does not have a problem with me – they have a problem with the prophet Isaiah!

> *Isaiah 9:6*
> *For unto us a child is born, unto us a son is given: and the government shall be upon his shoulder: and his name shall be called Wonderful, Counsellor, The mighty God, The everlasting Father, The Prince of Peace.*

Although this verse is quoted often, it seems the depth of truth found in it is often overlooked. This verse is clearly dealing with the Son which would be born, and yet it calls Him the Father!

How could One Individual be both Father and Son? Let me provide a few verses which might help to clarify this:

1. He can be both Father and Son in the same way that He can be both Alpha AND Omega, Beginning AND End, First AND Last.

> *Revelation 22:13*
> *I am Alpha and Omega, the beginning and the end, the first and the last.*

2. He can be both Father and Son in the same way that He can be both the Rose of Sharon AND the Lily of the Valleys.

> *Song of Solomon 2:1*
> *I am the rose of Sharon, and the lily of the valleys.*

3. He can be both Father and Son in the same way that He can be both the root of David AND the offspring of David.

> *Revelation 22:16*
> *I Jesus have sent mine angel to testify unto you these things in the churches. I am the root and the*

offspring of David, and the bright and morning star.

    a.   **I might add that this is also the answer to the question Jesus asked concerning how Christ could be both David's son AND his Lord.**

Luke 20:41-44
And he said unto them, How say they that Christ is David's son? ⁴²And David himself saith in the book of Psalms, The LORD said unto my Lord, Sit thou on my right hand, ⁴³Till I make thine enemies thy footstool. ⁴⁴David therefore calleth him Lord, how is he then his son?

    b.   He was David's son according to the flesh, but His Lord according to the Spirit!

4.   He can be both Father and Son in the same way that He can be both the Lion of the Tribe of Judah AND the Lamb of God.

Revelation 5:5
And one of the elders saith unto me, Weep not: behold, the Lion of the tribe of Juda, the Root of David, hath prevailed to open the book, and to loose the seven seals thereof.

John 1:29
The next day John seeth Jesus coming unto him, and saith, Behold the Lamb of God, which taketh away the sin of the world.

5.   He can be both Father and Son in the same way that He can be the High Priest AND the Sacrifice!

Hebrews 3:1
Wherefore, holy brethren, partakers of the heavenly calling, consider the Apostle and High Priest of our profession, Christ Jesus;

> **Hebrews 9:28**
> *So Christ was once offered to bear the sins of many; and unto them that look for him shall he appear the second time without sin unto salvation.*

Indeed, Jesus WAS both God and man, which means He was both Father and Son. In Him, humanity and Deity were fused, but not confused. When He assumed a human nature at His incarnation, he did not cease to be God. Now, however, in addition to being what he always was, Jehovah God assumed a human nature.

The One God (Who is a Spirit) took on a robe of flesh (called "the Son"). As Paul said, "God was in Christ." This explains the biblical concept of the Godhead fully and comprehensively! This is, then, the fourth (and final) principle in understanding the Godhead: ***THE ONE GOD (THE SPIRIT) WAS IN CHRIST (THE FLESH) IN THE PERSON OF JESUS.***

Before going any further in this study, there is something I feel I must address. I ask you to please get this straight – those who hold to this Biblical doctrine have often been misrepresented by our detractors. They claim we believe that the Father IS the Son, or that the man Christ Jesus was His own Father. Neither accusation is true. We see a clear distinction between the Father and the Son – but it is NOT a distinction in persons.

> ***John 14:10***
> *Believest thou not that I am in the Father, and the Father in me? the words that I speak unto you I speak not of myself: but the Father that dwelleth in me, he doeth the works.*

Remember that the Father is the Eternal, Invisible Spirit. Remember that the Son is the visible, fleshly robe which the Father took on. Since the Spirit is not the flesh, you cannot say that the Father IS the Son. What you CAN accurately say is that

God in Christ

He Who is the Father is also the Son.

This brings us to yet another major fallacy of the doctrine of the Trinity. By this, I mean the teaching that each "separate and distinct person" is "co-equal" with the other "separate and distinct persons." Nowhere did the Son say He was equal with the Father. Instead, He said quite the opposite.

> *John 14:28*
> *Ye have heard how I said unto you, I go away, and come again unto you. If ye loved me, ye would rejoice, because I said, I go unto the Father: for my Father is greater than I.*

Jesus' clear statement is contrary to the belief in two "co-equal" persons! For those who understand the Oneness of the Godhead, we have no problem with this verse – in fact, it further confirms our message! When we read Father, we think "Spirit" and when we read Son, we think "Flesh." Therefore, Jesus was simply saying, "My Spirit is greater than my flesh."

This is why we can say the Father is not the Son -- because the Spirit is not the Flesh. Yet the Father and Son are not two different persons. Just as you have flesh and spirit (which are distinct from one another), but your spirit and flesh do not make up two people, so it is with Christ Jesus. His flesh (the Son) was NOT His Spirit (the Father), yet they are not two persons.

I find it quite interesting that most Trinitarians would readily say that "Jesus is fully God" (although they refer to Him as "God the Son"). My question to them is this: If Jesus is "fully God," is there ANY title for God which does not apply to Jesus? If you can find any title of God which cannot be ascribed to Jesus, then Jesus is not "FULLY" God!

My next question is: Can you apply the title "God the FATHER" to Jesus? If not, then you cannot say that Jesus is "fully God."

I cannot begin to comprehend why it is so difficult for some to say that Jesus is both the Father and the Son. Jesus certainly had no problem doing so.

When Philip asked to see the Father, Jesus responded to his question with a question. By asking this question, Jesus emphatically claimed the title of "the Father."

> **John 14:9**
> *Jesus saith unto him, Have I been so long time with you, and yet hast thou not known me, Philip? he that hath seen me hath seen the Father; and how sayest thou then, Shew us the Father?*

Philip had not asked to see a representation of the Father. He did not say he wanted to see Someone Who bore the characteristics and qualities of the Father. He requested to SEE THE FATHER. In response, Jesus asked Philip how it was that Philip had spent so much time with Him and yet did not know Who He was. The answer was clear and concise: "When you have seen Me, you have seen the Father."

Perhaps one reason Jesus seemed to address this question so straightforwardly was because He had already identified Himself in this way some time earlier. Notice His statement recorded four chapters prior to Philip's enquiry.

> **John 10:30**
> *I and my Father are one.*

Jesus did not say, "I and the Father agree in one." He did not say, "I and the Father make up two of the three-in-one." He said, "I and my Father ARE one." How much clearer could He be?

The fact is, even earlier than His claim of Oneness with the Father recorded in Chapter 10, Jesus stated that it is essential that men believe that He is the Father!

> **John 8:24**
> *I said therefore unto you, that ye shall die in your sins: for if ye believe not that I am he, ye*

shall die in your sins.

The phrase "I am He" is actually just "I Am" in the original Greek. In other words, Jesus openly told the Jews that He was the I Am – the One Who had spoken to Moses from the burning bush! He was, of course, claiming to be the very God (the Father) Whom their ancestors had worshipped for centuries!

In case you do not see that in verse 24, just keep reading. Verses 25 and 27 explain it in such detail that there can be no doubt.

John 8:25
Then said they unto him, Who art thou? And Jesus saith unto them, Even the same that I said unto you from the beginning.

John 8:27
They understood not that he spake to them of the Father.

When they asked Him Who He was, He simply responded that He had consistently given them the same answer. As John wrote this story, he was divinely inspired to provide complete and definite clarification on the correct answer concerning Who Jesus was. Even though the Jews "understood not," John wanted to be sure his readers DID understand that Jesus' answer was that He was the Father!

In fact, it was His reiteration of this statement that angered the Jews to the point of wanting to stone Him!

John 8:56-59
Your father Abraham rejoiced to see my day: and he saw it, and was glad. ⁵⁷Then said the Jews unto him, Thou art not yet fifty years old, and hast thou seen Abraham? ⁵⁸Jesus said unto them, Verily, verily, I say unto you, Before Abraham was, I am. ⁵⁹Then took they up stones to cast at him: but Jesus hid himself, and went out of the

temple, going through the midst of them, and so passed by.

The Jews wanted to stone Him because (in their minds), He was a man trying to "make Himself God" (see John 10:33). Interestingly, they had it exactly backwards – this was God Who had made Himself a man!

1 Timothy 3:16
And without controversy great is the mystery of godliness: God was manifest in the flesh, justified in the Spirit, seen of angels, preached unto the Gentiles, believed on in the world, received up into glory.

By this time, it should be readily obvious to every reader that the Son of God in the New Testament was the fleshly manifestation of Jehovah God of the Old Testament. The Father and Son are not two separate persons. Rather, the Son was the visible image (flesh) of the invisible God (Spirit).

Colossians 1:15
Who is the image of the invisible God, the firstborn of every creature:

As I close this chapter, please allow me to provide you with a brief summary of the four Scriptural principles which explain the Godhead:

(1) There is only one God.

Deuteronomy 6:4
Hear, O Israel: The LORD our God is one LORD.

(2) God (the Father) is a Spirit.

John 4:24
God is a Spirit: and they that worship him must worship him in spirit and in truth.

(3) Christ (the Son) was born of Mary and was,

therefore, flesh.

> **Luke 1:35**
>
> And the angel answered and said unto her, The Holy Ghost shall come upon thee, and the power of the Highest shall overshadow thee: therefore also that holy thing which shall be born of thee shall be called the Son of God.

(4) God (the Spirit) was in Christ (the flesh).

> **2 Corinthians 5:19**
>
> To wit, that God was in Christ, reconciling the world unto himself, not imputing their trespasses unto them; and hath committed unto us the word of reconciliation.

Based on these four principles, it is clear that there are not three persons in the Godhead. While Trinitarians teach that Jesus is in the Godhead, the Apostle Paul taught no such concept.

> **Colossians 2:9**
>
> For in him dwelleth all the fulness of the Godhead bodily.

Instead of teaching that Jesus is in the Godhead, Paul said that the Godhead is in Jesus!

While Trinitarians say that Jesus is the "Second Person in the Godhead," Jesus never called Himself the "second" anything! However, He did say this:

> **Revelation 22:13**
>
> I am Alpha and Omega, the beginning and the end, the first and the last.

Let me conclude by saying that I prefer that others would not try to identify me as believing in "Jesus Only." This implies that I deny the Father and the Holy Ghost, which I do not. Rather, I prefer to identify what I believe as "Jesus EVERYTHING!"

CHAPTER 5
PROVIDING FURTHER PROOF

Anyone who understands, accepts, and applies the four principles set forth thus far should most certainly arrive at the true Scriptural perspective on the Godhead. I now want to focus on a few Bible passages which confirm the things I have written so far. In so doing, I hope to solidify in the minds of the reader the fact that the doctrine of the Trinity is contrary to true Biblical teaching. God is NOT "three separate and distinct persons." Rather, God is one Spirit Who manifest Himself in the fleshly body of the man Christ Jesus.

EXAMPLE 1: THE PLAN OF GOD

The Bible declares that God's plan of redemption was NOT an afterthought. The Lord was not shocked or surprised when Adam sinned in the garden. He knew it was coming and already had a plan in place whereby He would redeem mankind. This is the reason Jesus was called "the Lamb slain from the foundation of the world."

> ***Revelation 13:8***
> *And all that dwell upon the earth shall worship him, whose names are not written in the book of life of the Lamb slain from the foundation of the*

world.

Of course, He was not LITERALLY "slain" from the beginning. He was slain in the mind of God – in God's foreknowledge.

When the Apostle John wrote his gospel, he did so in part to disprove certain philosophies and false doctrines that had already arisen concerning the Person of Jesus Christ. In his opening statement, he emphatically declared Who Jesus was.

John 1:1
In the beginning was the Word, and the Word was with God, and the Word was God.

"Word" here is translated from the Greek word "logos," which denotes more than a term which is uttered. It speaks of reason, concepts, thoughts, doctrine, purpose, ideas, and the expression and completion of one's will. Vincent's Word Studies says that it expresses both an inward thought, and the outward form by which that thought is expressed.[7]

I think the best definition of "logos" is "a plan," or, more particularly a blueprint. In other words, it is a detailed plan upon which and by which a structure is built. Thus, the *Riggen Revised Version* would read, "In the beginning, God had a plan. The plan was with God, and the plan was God!"

Before God laid "the foundation of the world," He already had a plan whereby He would provide salvation to fallen man, but it required the shedding of blood.

Hebrews 9:22
And almost all things are by the law purged with blood; and without shedding of blood is no remission.

---

[7] VINCENT, M. R. (1924). *Word Studies in the New Testament.* New York, Scribner.

Inasmuch as God is a Spirit (which does not have blood), something had to happen in order for this plan to be fulfilled. Thankfully, John goes on in his Gospel to tell us what happened.

> *John 1:14*
> *And the Word was made flesh, and dwelt among us, (and we beheld his glory, the glory as of the only begotten of the Father,) full of grace and truth.*

The literal rendering of this verse is "The Word became flesh." In order for God – Who WAS the plan – to fulfill the plan, He was manifest (or made known) in flesh!

> *1 Timothy 3:16*
> *And without controversy great is the mystery of godliness: God was manifest in the flesh, justified in the Spirit, seen of angels, preached unto the Gentiles, believed on in the world, received up into glory.*

The God of Heaven did not cease to become what He had always been – the Eternal, Omnipresent, Omniscient, Omnipotent Spirit. Now, though, He became something else IN ADDITION to what He had always been. He became what we are so He could make us more like He is. In order to fulfill His plan, Divinity was clothed in humanity!

This was not a matter of one divine person sending another person. Rather, it was the ONLY Divine One taking upon Himself human flesh for the purpose of redeeming sinful man!

While so many people love to quote John 3:16 to explain God's love for us, I contend that we cannot understand John 3:16 without using 1 John 3:16 as the key. Let us compare what the apostle said in these two verses.

> *John 3:16*
> *For God so loved the world, that he gave his only begotten Son, that whosoever believeth in*

him should not perish, but have everlasting life.

1 John 3:16

Hereby perceive we the love of God, because he laid down his life for us: and we ought to lay down our lives for the brethren.

In his gospel, John quoted Jesus as saying that "God ... gave His ... Son." In his epistle, he stated that "God ... laid down HIS life for us." The only way we can interpret these two verses so that they do NOT contradict is to understand that the "Son" spoken of in John 3:16 was the fleshly body inhabited by God the Father! Indeed, God gave His Son and thereby laid down His own life.

Understanding that God manifesting Himself in a robe of flesh and then laying down that life to save us was the fulfillment of God's plan, one can more easily grasp Jesus' words in His prayer in the Upper Room. During that prayer, Jesus spoke about the glory He had "before the world was."

John 17:5

And now, O Father, glorify thou me with thine own self with the glory which I had with thee before the world was.

That "glory" was not as a second person coequal and coeternal with the Father. The glory the Son had from the foundation of the world was in the mind (*i.e.*, the foreknowledge) of God! It was a part of God's "logos" – His plan which was with Him in the beginning!

Please consider something, and be honest with yourself concerning the answer to the following question. How much love does it take for one person to send a different person to die? The answer is simple: it does not take nearly as much as if the person went himself! The Father did not tell the Son to go and die for us. The Father took upon Himself human flesh so that He Himself could do it! As John 1:1 says, "The [Plan] was God!" That, my friends, is TRUE love!

EXAMPLE 2: THE PROPHECY OF JOEL

On the day of Pentecost, when the amazed onlookers began doubting, questioning, and mocking what they saw, they began to ask, "What meaneth this?" (Acts 2:12). In response, Peter stated unequivocally that what had just happened was the fulfillment of Joel's prophecy.

Acts 2:14-18

But Peter, standing up with the eleven, lifted up his voice, and said unto them, Ye men of Judaea, and all ye that dwell at Jerusalem, be this known unto you, and hearken to my words: 15For these are not drunken, as ye suppose, seeing it is but the third hour of the day. 16But this is that which was spoken by the prophet Joel; 17And it shall come to pass in the last days, saith God, I will pour out of my Spirit upon all flesh: and your sons and your daughters shall prophesy, and your young men shall see visions, and your old men shall dream dreams: 18And on my servants and on my handmaidens I will pour out in those days of my Spirit; and they shall prophesy:

There can be no debate about the fact that this outpouring of God's Spirit was the very thing about which the Prophet Joel had written centuries before. With that being established, let us examine the prophecy itself.

Joel 2:28

And it shall come to pass afterward, that I will pour out my spirit upon all flesh; and your sons and your daughters shall prophesy, your old men shall dream dreams, your young men shall see visions:

You might immediately notice that what God said through Joel was that He would pour out His spirit "afterward." According

Providing Further Proof

to this prophecy, there was to be some event that would precede the Pentecostal outpouring. It would only come "afterward," but after what? The answer to that question lies in the previous verse.

> **Joel 2:27**
> And ye shall know that I am in the midst of Israel, and that I am the LORD your God, and none else: and my people shall never be ashamed.

Let us look closely at verse 27. "LORD" in the original is "Jehovah"[8] (the name by which God identified Himself to the patriarchs of the Old Testament), and "God" is "Elohim" (the term used to identify the Creator in Genesis 1:1). Therefore, this verse states that "Jehovah your Elohim" would be "in the midst of Israel."

Verse 28 then tells us that the Spirit would be poured out AFTER what was stated in verse 27 was accomplished; that is, AFTER Jehovah Elohim had been "in the midst of Israel." We know that God cannot lie (see Hebrews 6:18), so Jehovah Elohim MUST HAVE BEEN in the midst of Israel at some point BEFORE the Day of Pentecost.

The Jews certainly did not consider Jehovah Elohim to be a tri-unity of persons. They knew Him to be the One and Only God of Israel. Joel, writing under the inspiration of the Holy Ghost said it would be that very God Who would be present in Israel before His Spirit was poured out upon them.

Just prior to the event which Peter identified as the fulfillment of Joel 2:28, Jesus had literally been "in the midst of Israel."

---

[8] It should be noted that in most King James Bibles, when you read an Old Testament passage wherein the word "Lord" appears in all capitals (as it does in Joel 2:27), it was printed that way at the direction of the translators. They wanted to distinguish this word "Lord" from any other Hebrew word translated in the same way. When it appears in all capitals, it is so the reader can readily recognize that the original word used was the word we now pronounce as "Jehovah."

Understanding the Godhead

Accordingly, it should be obvious that Jesus was none other than "Jehovah Elohim!" He was not "Jehovah, Jr." – He was Jehovah Elohim!

That Jesus is Jehovah Elohim is confirmed in the writings of the Old Testament prophets. One example is found in Zechariah.

> ***Zechariah 12:10***
> *And I will pour upon the house of David, and upon the inhabitants of Jerusalem, the spirit of grace and of supplications: and they shall look upon me whom they have pierced, and they shall mourn for him, as one mourneth for his only son, and shall be in bitterness for him, as one that is in bitterness for his firstborn.*

The One speaking through Zechariah says that the day will come in which "they shall look upon ME whom they have pierced." This Speaker had already identified Himself in the first few verses of the chapter.

> ***Zechariah 12:1***
> *The burden of the word of the LORD for Israel, saith the LORD, which stretcheth forth the heavens, and layeth the foundation of the earth, and formeth the spirit of man within him.*

Just as was the case in Joel 2:27, the word "Lord" is actually "Jehovah." Jehovah was the One who "stretcheth forth the heavens, and layeth the foundation of the earth, and formeth the spirit of man within him." In other words, Jehovah is simply another name for the Elohim of Genesis 1!

When you take Zechariah 12:1 (where Jehovah says He created everything) and combine it with verse 10 (where He says that HE will be pierced), you can come to only one rational conclusion. These verses show us beyond the shadow of a doubt that One Who would be pierced was Jehovah Elohim. That One, Jesus Christ, was none other than the Creator of the Universe – the

Providing Further Proof

One and Only True God!

EXAMPLE 3: JEHOVAH, MY SAVIOR

In this third example, we will build on the same premise as found in the previous one. This time we hope to provide an even clearer identification for the Jehovah of the Old Testament.

To do this, let us begin with something found in the Book of Exodus. Immediately after their deliverance from the Egyptians, Moses and the children of Israel sang an interesting song.

> ***Exodus 15:2***
>
> *The LORD is my strength and song, and he is become my salvation: he is my God, and I will prepare him an habitation; my father's God, and I will exalt him.*

In their chorus of thanksgiving and praise, Moses and the Children of Israel spoke of Jehovah (notice that the word "Lord" is in all capitals) as their strength and their song. Then, they sang together that "He [Jehovah] is become my salvation." This same statement is made twice in the Book of Psalms.

> ***Psalms 118:14***
>
> *The LORD is my strength and song, and is become my salvation.*

> ***Psalms 118:21***
>
> *I will praise thee: for thou hast heard me, and art become my salvation.*

Moses and the Psalmist were not the only ones to describe Jehovah in this way. Twice in one verse Isaiah speaks of it as well.

> ***Isaiah 12:2***
>
> *Behold, God is my salvation; I will trust, and not be afraid: for the LORD JEHOVAH is my strength and my song; he also is become my salvation.*

Looking at the original Hebrew, there is a beautiful insight into these verses that our English Bible has hidden from us. The word "salvation" in each of the above-mentioned passages is the Hebrew word "Yeshua."

If that word sounds familiar, it is no wonder – it is the very name given to the Messiah! You see, "Yeshua" is the Hebrew form of the English name "Jesus."

With that in mind, let us go back and consider exactly what was said. In Exodus 15:2, Psalm 118:14, and Psalm 118:21, we find: "Jehovah is my strength and song, and He is become my Jesus!"

In Isaiah 12:2, we read, "Behold, God is my Jesus; I will trust, and not be afraid: for JEHOVAH is my strength and my song; he also is become my Jesus!" How much clearer can it be?

EXAMPLE 4: THE HEAVENLY THRONE

In our final example, we jump to the last book of the New Testament, the Book of Revelation. Here, we read of a time in which John was given a glimpse into Heaven. Our example is based on what he saw.

Revelation 4:2
And immediately I was in the spirit: and, behold, a throne was set in heaven, and one sat on the throne.

John saw ONE throne and ONE sitting on the throne. Concerning this verse, one commentator wrote, "It is not easy to determine who is meant. That the Sitter on the throne is neither Jesus nor the Holy Spirit is indeed obvious ... But is He the Father or the Triune God?"[9]

---

[9] SCHAFF, P. (1883). *A Popular Commentary on the New Testament.* Edinburgh, T. & T. Clark.

Providing Further Proof

I cannot figure out why it seems so "obvious" that the "Sitter" is not Jesus. Furthermore, how could the "Sitter" (singular) be the "Triune God" (three persons) sitting on ONE throne? As I mentioned in the Introduction, reading what the scholars who adhere to the Trinitarian doctrine write, one begins to understand why they come to the conclusion that it is a "mystery beyond comprehension!"

Since there was only ONE throne, it seems to me it would be very crowded if the members of the Trinity are all sitting on the same one. The fact is that John saw exactly the same thing Isaiah had seen centuries before – one throne and One seated on that throne.

Isaiah 6:1
In the year that king Uzziah died I saw also the Lord sitting upon a throne, high and lifted up, and his train filled the temple.

Isaiah, like John, saw ONE sitting upon "**A** throne," (*i.e.*, ONE throne)! The One Isaiah saw on that throne was identified in verse 3.

Isaiah 6:3
And one cried unto another, and said, Holy, holy, holy, is the LORD of hosts: the whole earth is full of his glory.

Isaiah saw Jehovah on the throne. It should be evident, then, that the One John saw sitting on that throne would also be Jehovah. In fact, the angels were quoted in Revelation as praising the One on the throne with the same words Isaiah heard them say.

Revelation 4:8
And the four beasts had each of them six wings about him; and they were full of eyes within: and they rest not day and night, saying, Holy, holy, holy, Lord God Almighty, which was, and is, and is to come.

In order to help the above-mentioned author, perhaps it should also be pointed out that both verses 9 and 10 refer to the "Sitter" by using the singular pronoun. The angelic creatures are NOT worshipping "them," they are worshipping HIM!

> ***Revelation 4:9-11***
>
> *And when those beasts give glory and honour and thanks to him that sat on the throne, who liveth for ever and ever, ¹⁰The four and twenty elders fall down before him that sat on the throne, and worship him that liveth for ever and ever, and cast their crowns before the throne, saying, ¹¹Thou art worthy, O Lord, to receive glory and honour and power: for thou hast created all things, and for thy pleasure they are and were created.*

If the "Sitter" on the throne was "the Triune God," then Revelation 5 presents a REAL problem. If three divine persons (Father, Son, and Holy Ghost) were seated on Heaven's throne, then WHO, pray tell, is the One that takes the book and is called "the Lion of the Tribe of Juda" and "the Root of David?" If the Son is among the three seated, then He cannot be the one taking the book, even though verse 6 calls Him the "Lamb!"

> ***Revelation 5:1-9***
>
> *And I saw in the right hand of him that sat on the throne a book written within and on the backside, sealed with seven seals. ²And I saw a strong angel proclaiming with a loud voice, Who is worthy to open the book, and to loose the seals thereof? ³And no man in heaven, nor in earth, neither under the earth, was able to open the book, neither to look thereon. ⁴And I wept much, because no man was found worthy to open and to read the book, neither to look thereon. ⁵And one of the elders saith unto me, Weep not: behold, the Lion of the tribe of Juda, the Root of David, hath prevailed to open the book, and to loose the seven*

CHAPTER 6
QUESTIONS ANSWERED

In this chapter, I want to address some of the questions which I have been asked by those who believe in the Trinity. I believe it is imperative (in fact, I see it as an apostolic mandate) that we be prepared to provide answers to those who seek them in sincerity.

The reason I refer to this as "an apostolic mandate" is because of something Peter wrote in his epistle. You see, the Apostle Peter instructed us to "be ready always to give an answer to every man."

> ***1 Peter 3:15***
> *But sanctify the Lord God in your hearts: and be ready always to give an answer to every man that asketh you a reason of the hope that is in you with meekness and fear:*

Dr. Albert Barnes said that the phrase "be ready always" means that we should "(a) Be always able to do it; have such reasons for the hope that is in you that they can be stated; or, have good and substantial reasons; and, (b) Be willing to state those reasons on all proper occasions."[10]

In other words, we have a responsibility to apply ourselves to

---

[10] BARNES, A., Murphy, J. G., Cook, F. C., Pusey, E. B., Leupold, H. C., & Frew, R., (1996). *Barnes' Notes.* Grand Rapids, Michigan: Baker.

"I found it necessary to write to you and urge you to continue your vigorous defense of the faith."[12]

Hence, the purpose of this chapter is to help equip those who embrace the Biblical truth concerning the Godhead. Of course, it is also intended to instruct (or refute) those who do not.

QUESTION 1: THE PLURALITY OF NOUNS AND PRONOUNS

Trinitarians often like to point out that one of the more common Hebrew titles for God is "Elohim," which is actually a plural form of the word "El," meaning "God." Its plurality cannot be denied; in fact, the word is sometimes translated as "gods."

While they are correct in their assessment, the mistake they make is in assuming that the use of a plural noun MUST be indicative of (in this case) a plurality of persons in the Godhead. Obviously, this is NOT the case.

The term "Elohim" was not only used to refer to Jehovah. It was also used in reference to Baal and Beelzebub.

> ### *Judges 6:31*
> *And Joash said unto all that stood against him, Will ye plead for Baal? will ye save him? he that will plead for him, let him be put to death whilst it is yet morning: if he be a god, let him plead for himself, because one hath cast down his altar.*

> ### *2 Kings 1:2*
> *And Ahaziah fell down through a lattice in his upper chamber that was in Samaria, and was sick: and he sent messengers, and said unto them, Go, enquire of Baalzebub the god of Ekron*

---

[12] DAVIDSON PRESS. (2003). The Holy Bible: International Standard Version: New Testament. Yorba Linda, CA, Davidson Press.

Questions Answered

whether I shall recover of this disease.

In both of these verses, the word "god" (referring to Baal in Judges and Baalzebub in 2 Kings) was translated from the plural word "Elohim." Is one to suppose that the god of the Canaanites and the god of the Philistines were ALSO each a "Trinity?" Of course not!

Furthermore, as I have already pointed out, prophecies which spoke directly about Jesus also used "Elohim." To prove this, let us again look to the Prophet Zechariah.

Zechariah 11:4
Thus saith the LORD my God; Feed the flock of the slaughter;

Notice Who is identified as the Speaker in Zechariah's prophecy. The literal translation is, "Thus says Jehovah my Elohim."

When we get to verses 11 and 12 in this chapter, then, it is STILL Elohim Who is speaking. Yet notice what He says will happen to Him.

Zechariah 11:12-13
And I said unto them, If ye think good, give me my price; and if not, forbear. So they weighed for my price thirty pieces of silver. ¹³And the LORD said unto me, Cast it unto the potter: a goodly price that I was prised at of them. And I took the thirty pieces of silver, and cast them to the potter in the house of the LORD.

Were three Persons sold for thirty pieces of silver? NO! Clearly the use of "Elohim" was a reference to Jesus – NOT to a Trinity!

Three chapters later, Zechariah wrote about something else God would do. Note that it will be done as "Elohim."

> **Zechariah 14:5**
>
> *And ye shall flee to the valley of the mountains; for the valley of the mountains shall reach unto Azal: yea, ye shall flee, like as ye fled from before the earthquake in the days of Uzziah king of Judah: and the LORD my God shall come, and all the saints with thee.*

Are three Persons coming back? Again, the answer is a resounding, "NO!" The reason we can be so adamant about the fact that only ONE is coming back, is because that is exactly the way the Apostle Paul said it would be.

> **1 Thessalonians 3:13**
>
> *To the end he may stablish your hearts unblameable in holiness before God, even our Father, at the coming of our Lord Jesus Christ with all his saints.*

Since the use of the plural noun "Elohim" clearly does not indicate a plurality of persons in the passages above, one is left to ask what it DOES indicate. The answer is that it implies a plurality of majesty.

Remember that the Jews have used the term "Elohim" for centuries and have NEVER understood it to indicate a plurality in the Godhead. How is it that Christians should be so arrogant as to try to tell THEM what THEIR language means? The very idea is laughable!

The plurality found in Elohim is used to signify the fact that God is far greater in majesty and glory than what can be described in singular terms. The vastness of His power and kingdom dictate that He be shown a respect that exceeds what can be shown to even the greatest of human beings. In order to reflect that concept, the Old Testament writer was often inspired to describe this One Lord of Deuteronomy 6:4 in plural terms. It is as simple as that.

Along these same lines, let us consider something closely

Questions Answered

related. I have not only been asked many times about the use of the plural noun "Elohim," but many more times about the use of the plural pronouns found in the story of creation.

> **Genesis 1:26**
> *And God said, Let us make man in our image, after our likeness: and let them have dominion over the fish of the sea, and over the fowl of the air, and over the cattle, and over all the earth, and over every creeping thing that creepeth upon the earth.*

Based on this verse, the argument is often made that since God spoke using plural pronouns, there must be more than one person in the Godhead. While there are many differing opinions on the use of the plural pronouns in this passage, I will personally stick with the most simple one (which I also happen to believe is the correct one).

Just as we learned that the plural noun "Elohim" does not require a plurality of persons, so we should understand the same principle is true concerning plural pronouns. The use of plural pronouns do not show one member of the Trinity speaking to others; rather, God was using what is known as a "majestic plural."

For centuries, if a ruler greeted a crowd, he would not say, "I am happy to be here;" rather, he would say, "We are happy to be here." The plurality used was not one of persons, but of majesty – the one speaking spoke on behalf of the entire kingdom they represented.

Interestingly, this usage is still practiced in much of Africa. If, for example, they want to show the highest respect to an elder, they do not refer to that individual as "him" or "her;" instead, they refer to "them," even though there is only one person being referenced.

Thankfully, you do not have to simply take my word for the

fact that the use of "us" and "our" do not indicate a conversation between multiple persons. One only has to go to the very next verse in Genesis to further confirm the explanation I have provided.

> **Genesis 1:27**
> So God created man in his own image, in the image of God created he him; male and female created he them.

Notice that this verse does NOT say, "created THEY him," but "created HE him." Although God spoke in plurality, He acted in singularity!

I would like to say at this point that, in spite of how some people view this verse, I do not believe God was consulting with the angels. He did not say, "Watch Me make man." He said "Let US make man," which would signify that He would be inviting them to participate in the creation. The Scripture clearly says this did NOT happen, inasmuch as the Book of Isaiah informs us that ONE Being served as Creator.

> **Isaiah 44:24**
> Thus saith the LORD, thy redeemer, and he that formed thee from the womb, I am the LORD that maketh all things; that stretcheth forth the heavens alone; that spreadeth abroad the earth by myself;

Jehovah unequivocally stated that He acted alone. He did not require nor request the input or assistance of any other being – angelic or otherwise. He did it BY HIMSELF.

QUESTION 2: WHAT HAPPENED ON JORDAN'S BANKS

It is often said that what took place when Jesus was baptized is absolute proof that three persons coexist in the Godhead. A close examination of the passage, however, will show that this is

Questions Answered

definitely NOT the case.

> **Matthew 3:16-17**
>
> *And Jesus, when he was baptized, went up straightway out of the water: and, lo, the heavens were opened unto him, and he saw the Spirit of God descending like a dove, and lighting upon him: [17]And lo a voice from heaven, saying, This is my beloved Son, in whom I am well pleased.*

To begin with, please note that John did NOT see three Persons. He saw only ONE Person – the One he was baptizing. Other than that One, he saw ONE Spirit (NOT A PERSON) which descended like a dove, and heard ONE voice.

All of this happened, according to John's own testimony, as proof to him that Christ was the Messiah. It was NOT intended to try to establish a doctrine about the number of persons in the Godhead!

> **John 1:33-34**
>
> *And I knew him not: but he that sent me to baptize with water, the same said unto me, Upon whom thou shalt see the Spirit descending, and remaining on him, the same is he which baptizeth with the Holy Ghost. [34]And I saw, and bare record that this is the Son of God.*

In trying to use this passage to make light of the doctrine of the Oneness of God, someone once asked, "Was Jesus a ventriloquist?" Someone else queried, "Was Heaven empty when Jesus was on earth?" The answer to both questions is NO!

> **John 3:13**
>
> *And no man hath ascended up to heaven, but he that came down from heaven, even the Son of man which is in heaven.*

In John 3, Jesus told Nicodemus that, while He was on earth, He was still in Heaven at the same time! Although the fleshly body

Understanding the Godhead

was on earth, the Spirit that indwelt that body still filled the heavens, for that Spirit is OMNIPRESENT! There was no need for Jesus to "throw His voice," and there has never been a time when Heaven was "empty." Since He was both in Heaven (as the Spirit) and on earth (as the flesh), then He could be in the water AND speaking from Heaven all at once!

QUESTION 3: THE USE OF VERBS SUCH AS "SENT" OR "GAVE"

Trinitarians make much ado over verses which speak of the Father SENDING the Son or the Father GIVING the Son. They claim that the use of words like "sent" or "gave" prove Christ pre-existed prior to Bethlehem. A few examples ought to suffice for clarification of this point.

> *John 6:40*
>
> *And this is the will of him that sent me, that every one which seeth the Son, and believeth on him, may have everlasting life: and I will raise him up at the last day.*
>
> *John 3:16*
>
> *For God so loved the world, that he gave his only begotten Son, that whosoever believeth in him should not perish, but have everlasting life.*

To them, it is not possible for God to "send" His Son unless His Son was already present with the Father. Likewise, they insist that the Father could not "give" His Son without the Son existing prior to being given.

This may sound logical at first glance. If it is true, though, we run into a serious problem when considering a few verses which use this same terminology.

> *John 1:6*
>
> *There was a man sent from God, whose name*

Questions Answered

was John.

The Bible says that God "sent" John. Does anyone believe that John the Baptist somehow existed prior to his birth? I hope not. Obviously, he was "sent" many years AFTER he was born!

> **Genesis 17:15-16**
>
> *And God said unto Abraham, As for Sarai thy wife, thou shalt not call her name Sarai, but Sarah shall her name be. ¹⁶And I will bless her, and give thee a son also of her: yea, I will bless her, and she shall be a mother of nations; kings of people shall be of her.*

God told Abraham he would be "given" a son. Did Isaac pre-exist? Of course not!

> **Genesis 48:9**
>
> *And Joseph said unto his father, They are my sons, whom God hath given me in this place. And he said, Bring them, I pray thee, unto me, and I will bless them.*

Joseph told Jacob that God "gave" his sons to him. Did Joseph's sons exist before they were born? I think you get the picture.

Obviously, trying to use the verbs "sent," "gave," and such like to prove there was a preexistent Son Who was with the Father in eternity is an exercise in futility. These words prove no such concept.

I have already shown in a previous chapter that the Son of God (the humanity) was "made of a woman" (see Galatians 4:4), and was, in fact, begotten on a particular day (see Hebrews 1:5). It is impossible for Him to be the Eternal Son and the Begotten Son (see John 3:16) at the same time.

Understanding the Godhead

QUESTION 4: THE FACT THAT JESUS PRAYED

People who cling to their traditional ideas of the Godhead will sometimes use examples of Jesus praying to prove that He was NOT the Father. One such example is, of course, His prayer in the Garden of Gethsemane.

> *Matthew 26:39*
> *And he went a little further, and fell on his face, and prayed, saying, O my Father, if it be possible, let this cup pass from me: nevertheless not as I will, but as thou wilt.*

To Trinitarians, the fact that Jesus prayed to the Father proves they were two separate persons. The problem is not only that they are wrong on THAT point, but this very example contradicts the basic premise of the Trinitarian doctrine!

The reason I say that is because they teach that the Father and Son are co-equal and, as such, both are omnipotent. However, if the Son was equal to the Father, and was omnipotent AS THE SON, why would He seek the help of One Who was only as powerful as He Himself was? The very fact that the man Christ Jesus prayed to the Father PROVES He was not "coequal with" the Father!

Make no mistake: this passage does NOT show one person in the Godhead praying to another person. What it shows is the flesh praying to Spirit!

Just two verses after stating that Jesus prayed to the Father, Matthew quoted something Jesus said to His disciples. This quote helps to explain my response to the question at hand.

> *Matthew 26:41*
> *Watch and pray, that ye enter not into temptation: the spirit indeed is willing, but the flesh is weak.*

When applied to the person of Jesus Christ, we can draw a

concise conclusion. The Spirit (the Father) was willing, but the flesh (the Son) was weak. In fact, Jesus said in another place that the Father (Spirit) was GREATER THAN (not "coequal to") the Son (flesh).

> **John 14:28**
> Ye have heard how I said unto you, I go away, and come again unto you. If ye loved me, ye would rejoice, because I said, I go unto the Father: for my Father is greater than I.

QUESTION 5: THE FATHER KNOWS WHAT THE SON DOES NOT

My wife and I were at a meeting several years ago where the people in charge chose to close with prayer. The man who prayed that closing prayer made a statement while praying that caught my attention. As he prayed, he said, "Father Jesus ..." and then went on to make his petition.

I decided to try to find the man afterwards and find out if that statement was an accident, or if he truly believed that Jesus IS the Father. When I finally located him, he was surrounded by some of his friends, who were all laughing loudly.

Eventually they noticed that I was standing there and began regaining their composure. I introduced myself to the man who had prayed and asked him about what he had said. His friends again started laughing as he turned bright red. One of the men standing close by proceeded to tell me that his wording was the cause of their laughter. They were making fun of him for calling the Father "Jesus," and made sure I knew none of them believed such a thing.

The laughing came to an abrupt halt when I informed them that, unlike them, I DO believe the name of the Father is Jesus. They stared at me for a moment, and then someone else standing nearby spoke up.

"I used to wonder about that Oneness doctrine," he said, "until I read where the Father knows the time of the Son's return, but the Son does not." He continued, "I realized right then that there was no way they could be the same if the Father knows something the Son does not."

The verse of which the man spoke is found in Mark's gospel. I include it here for reference.

Mark 13:32
But of that day and that hour knoweth no man, no, not the angels which are in heaven, neither the Son, but the Father.

My response to the man was akin to the explanation I offered earlier with regard to Jesus praying. I said, "That verse is more problematic for you as a Trinitarian than it is for me." I then proceeded to explain to him that the doctrine of the Trinity states that the Father and Son are coequal. I asked, "If the Father and Son are equal with each other, how can one know something the other does not? That sure does not sound very 'equal' to me!" This certainly does not sound like two co-equal omniscient Persons to me!

Of course the Son (humanity) is NOT equal to the Father (Divinity). As I just stated a few paragraphs back, Jesus said that the Father (Spirit) is greater than the Son (Flesh). As such, the Father (Spirit) can obviously know things the Son (Flesh) does not.

In addressing the man who had been let down through the roof, Jesus forgave his sins. Some of those present begin to think within themselves that Jesus had committed blasphemy by doing so. Mark then tells us not only that Jesus knew their thoughts, but he specifically states HOW He knew.

Mark 2:8
And immediately when Jesus perceived in his spirit that they so reasoned within themselves, he

said unto them, Why reason ye these things in your hearts?

According to Mark, Jesus "perceived in His Spirit." The word "perceived" is translated from the Greek word "epiginoosko," which can also be translated as "knew." In other words, the way Jesus was able to respond to their thoughts was because He "knew in the Spirit" what they were thinking. This was not a knowledge He gained through His flesh; He only knew it in the Spirit.

The same thing is true concerning the day and hour of His return. He did not have that knowledge based on His flesh, but in His Spirit, He knew all things (see John 21:17).

QUESTION 6: MAKING INTERCESSION

After teaching on the Godhead in my seminars in Africa, I always provide time for those in attendance to ask questions. When doing so, I have found that almost invariably I will be asked the same few questions at each location to which I travel. It has become so common that I have begun answering those questions before I open the floor to any others. Virtually without exception, I will be asked one or more of the five preceding questions I have listed here, or one or both of the two that follow this one.

There was one occasion when I was asked a question I had never been asked. I was thrilled! To me, it showed that someone was not just relying on the same old traditions they had always been taught, but they were doing some studying of their own.

Based on my experience, if one person asks a question, there are generally a number of others who would also like to know the answer. It is for that reason I am including this question within the pages of this book.

The question I was asked that day involves a principle which is addressed in a couple of different passages. I will list two of them so you can better understand the basis for the question.

Romans 8:34
> Who is he that condemneth? It is Christ that died, yea rather, that is risen again, who is even at the right hand of God, who also maketh intercession for us.

Hebrews 7:25
> Wherefore he is able also to save them to the uttermost that come unto God by him, seeing he ever liveth to make intercession for them.

Because of these verses, Trinitarians claim the Second Person is making intercession to the First Person on our behalf. Of course that is not at all the case.

To begin with, Jesus plainly and openly stated that all we have to do is ask Him directly. He then promised He Himself would answer.

John 14:14
> If ye shall ask any thing in my name, I will do it.

Furthermore, we cannot overlook what Paul wrote to the church at Rome concerning this process of "intercession" prior to the statement in verse 34 (which is quoted above). In verses 26 and 27, the apostle had already explained how intercession actually takes place.

Romans 8:26-27
> Likewise the Spirit also helpeth our infirmities: for we know not what we should pray for as we ought: but the Spirit itself maketh intercession for us with groanings which cannot be uttered. [27]And he that searcheth the hearts knoweth what is the mind of the Spirit, because he maketh intercession for the saints according to the will of God.

Questions Answered

Paul said that this intercession takes place when "the Spirit itself" does so. This is accomplished through "groanings which cannot be uttered." The Bible in Basic English translates this as: "the Spirit puts our desires into words which are not in our power to say."[13] According to verse 26, we often do not know exactly WHAT we should pray for, but, verse 27 tells us that when the Spirit begins to intercede THROUGH us, the Spirit will do so "according to the will of God."

Thus, the process of intercession is not a matter of one Divine Person interceding to another Divine Person on our behalf. Rather, it is a matter of the Spirit of God praying through us, helping us not to "ask amiss" (see James 4:3).

This is what Paul described in his first letter to the Corinthians. There, he referred to it as "praying in tongues" or "praying with the Spirit."

> *1 Corinthians 14:14-15*
>
> *For if I pray in an unknown tongue, my spirit prayeth, but my understanding is unfruitful. [15]What is it then? I will pray with the spirit, and I will pray with the understanding also: I will sing with the spirit, and I will sing with the understanding also.*

QUESTION 7: WHAT STEPHEN SAW IN HIS VISION

Another passage that is often cited as "absolute proof" of the Trinity is Acts 7. Trinitarians claim Stephen said he saw God AND Jesus during the vision he had prior to his death.

> *Acts 7:55*
>
> *But he, being full of the Holy Ghost, looked up stedfastly into heaven, and saw the glory of God,*

---

[13] HOOKE, S. H. (1982). *The Bible in Basic English.* Cambridge, Cambridge University Press.

and Jesus standing on the right hand of God,

If you pay attention to the wording of this verse, you discover Stephen made no such claim. Stephen indeed saw SOMETHING, but he did NOT see the Father AND the Son.

In order to prove this, let us begin with one of the first things we learned about God. In my discussion of the four principles needed to understand the Godhead, I showed from the Scripture that God the Father is a Spirit, and that Spirit is invisible – He cannot be seen!

John 1:18

No man hath seen God at any time; the only begotten Son, which is in the bosom of the Father, he hath declared him.

1 John 4:12

No man hath seen God at any time. If we love one another, God dwelleth in us, and his love is perfected in us.

1 Timothy 6:16

Who only hath immortality, dwelling in the light which no man can approach unto; whom no man hath seen, nor can see: to whom be honour and power everlasting. Amen.

Please pay particular attention to the last verse, which was written by Paul. The reason this is important is because Paul (then called "Saul") was standing there when Stephen had his vision!

Acts 7:58

And cast him out of the city, and stoned him: and the witnesses laid down their clothes at a young man's feet, whose name was Saul.

Acts 8:1

And Saul was consenting unto his death. And at that time there was a great persecution against the church which was at Jerusalem; and they

Questions Answered

were all scattered abroad throughout the regions of Judaea and Samaria, except the apostles.

In fact, it was evidently that very incident which put Paul under conviction. There was no way Paul could have forgotten about this incident, and yet he later wrote that "NO MAN HATH SEEN, NOR CAN SEE" God!

Since that obviously included Stephen, it is clear that Paul KNEW Stephen did NOT see two Persons! What Stephen DID see was "the glory of God, and Jesus standing on the right hand of God."

Of course, someone will ask, "How could someone see Jesus on God's right hand without also seeing God?" The answer to that question comes based on something else we learned about God – He is omnipresent.

Please tell me, if you can, where is the "right hand" of an OMNIPRESENT Spirit? Consider the air – can you stand on the right side or left side of the air? Obviously, "the right hand of God" is not a physical place. Rather, it is a metaphor for power.

It is an important practice to always allow Scripture to interpret Scripture. We will employ that necessary principle now, by examining the words Jesus Himself spoke when standing before Pilate.

Matthew 26:64
Jesus saith unto him, Thou hast said: nevertheless I say unto you, Hereafter shall ye see the Son of man sitting on the right hand of power, and coming in the clouds of heaven.

Mark 14:62
And Jesus said, I am: and ye shall see the Son of man sitting on the right hand of power, and coming in the clouds of heaven.

Jesus spoke of the day in which He would be seated "on the right hand of power." The Jews had long used the right hand to symbolize power, just as they did after the crossing of the Red Sea.

> **Exodus 15:6**
> *Thy right hand, O LORD, is become glorious in power: thy right hand, O LORD, hath dashed in pieces the enemy.*

Were the Children of Israel claiming they had seen God's palm and fingers doing this work? Absolutely not! Instead, they were simply claiming this victory had been the result of God's power.

Stephen did not see two Persons. What he saw was the glory of God and Jesus enthroned in all of God's power!

So many times in passages like this one, people get hung up on one verse without continuing to read the remaining verses. In so doing, they often miss a point of clarification offered within the verses themselves.

Such is the case with Stephen's vision. Pay attention to the prayer he prayed just four verses after describing what he saw.

> **Acts 7:59**
> *And they stoned Stephen, calling upon God, and saying, Lord Jesus, receive my spirit.*

As Stephen was dying, He called upon **God**. When he did, he only addressed One Being, and that was the "Lord Jesus!"

QUESTION 8: FORSAKEN BY THE FATHER

The final question which I will address in this book is perhaps my favorite of them all. Because of that, I have saved this one for last.

This question is based on what Jesus cried from the cross while He was dying. To some, it seems to prove a difference in the person of the Son from the Father. They claim that the Father

Questions Answered

showed us His great love by forsaking the Son (to the point of turning His face from Him, or as one man put it, "he averted his eyes from his Son"[14]) and allowing His Son to die.

> **Matthew 27:46**
> *And about the ninth hour Jesus cried with a loud voice, saying, Eli, Eli, lama sabachthani? that is to say, My God, my God, why hast thou forsaken me?*

Once again we find a passage which Trinitarians think helps them defend their beliefs when it actually proves them wrong. If the Son was coequal with the Father, why did it matter that the Father would forsake the Son? Furthermore, if the Father is such a loving God (which He is!), how could He possibly "forsake" His own Son?

To begin with, I do not believe that Jesus Christ was ever forsaken by God! (I will prove this from the Scripture at the conclusion of this section.)

What was happening here was the result of Christ becoming sin for us. Accordingly, He felt the touch of that which He had never felt before – the effects of sin.

> **2 Corinthians 5:21**
> *For he hath made him to be sin for us, who knew no sin; that we might be made the righteousness of God in him.*

He, standing in the stead of sinners, felt what every sinner feels. He FELT separated from God. I must be clear, however: Although Christ FELT God-forsaken, that was NOT the case.

---

[14] DEVER, M., DUNCAN, J. L., MOHLER JR., R. A., MAHANEY, C. J., PIPER, J., SPROUL, R. C., MACARTHUR, J., & ANYABWILE, T. M. (2009). *Proclaiming a Cross-centered Theology*. Wheaton, IL, Crossway.

Why, then, did Christ speak those words? To help you get a clearer understanding of the purpose behind His cry, consider something for a moment: If I say, "Amazing Grace, how sweet the sound," what comes to mind?

I have little doubt your response is: "That saved a wretch like me." The reason those particular words came to mind is because you are familiar with the words of that song.

If I say, "The Lord is my shepherd," what comes to mind? I am sure the answer you gave is, "I shall not want." Once again, the reason those words came to mind was because you are familiar with the words of that Psalm!

With that in mind, consider the fact that "My God, my God, why hast thou forsaken me?" was not just a phrase uttered by our Savior as He died. Those are the first words in the first verse of Psalm 22.

> **Psalm 22:1**
> *My God, my God, why hast thou forsaken me? why art thou so far from helping me, and from the words of my roaring?*

At the very moment in which the Son FELT God-forsaken, He began to sing (remember, the Psalms made up the song book of Israel) the Psalm which described what He felt. When He did, every Jew standing near enough to hear must surely have begun reciting the remainder of that passage in their minds, if not aloud. As they did, they were forced to realize that Psalm 22 was being fulfilled before their very eyes.

Consider a few sample verses:

> **Psalm 22:6-8**
> *But I am a worm, and no man; a reproach of men, and despised of the people. ⁷All they that see me laugh me to scorn: they shoot out the lip, they shake the head saying, ⁸He trusted on the LORD that he would deliver him: let him deliver him,*

Questions Answered

> *seeing he delighted in him.*

What was being said at the cross? According to Matthew, the crowd around the cross were saying the very words written in Psalm 22 centuries before!

> **Matthew 27:43**
> *He trusted in God; let him deliver him now, if he will have him: for he said, I am the Son of God.*

Let us continue reading through this Psalm. As we do, we will begin to realize there is no clearer picture of a man being crucified than what is recorded in these verses.

> **Psalm 22:13-16**
> *They gaped upon me with their mouths, as a ravening and a roaring lion. ^{14}I am poured out like water, and all my bones are out of joint: my heart is like wax; it is melted in the midst of my bowels. ^{15}My strength is dried up like a potsherd; and my tongue cleaveth to my jaws; and thou hast brought me into the dust of death. ^{16}For dogs have compassed me: the assembly of the wicked have inclosed me: they pierced my hands and my feet.*

Notice what is written: His bones were out of joint; His strength was dried up; His tongue was cleaving to the roof of His mouth; His hands and feet were pierced! Can there be any doubt that this prophecy was being fulfilled at Calvary?

Yet we are not finished. Pay attention to one more thing the Psalmist said would happen that DID happen during our Lord's crucifixion.

> **Psalm 22:17-18**
> *I may tell all my bones: they look and stare upon me. ^{18}They part my garments among them, and cast lots upon my vesture.*

There is no way anyone could argue that Psalm 22 was

anything other than a prophetic song about the death of the Savior. In fact, Matthew specifically quotes these verses to further prove Jesus was the Messiah.

> **Matthew 27:35**
> And they crucified him, and parted his garments, casting lots: that it might be fulfilled which was spoken by the prophet, They parted my garments among them, and upon my vesture did they cast lots.

It is my contention that Jesus looked upon the very crowd that had ordered His death and, in a final moment of love and compassion, used the words of this centuries-old Psalm to try to reach the hearts of those who hated Him. In His matchless mercy and grace, He began to sing as though for one last altar call. He obviously hoped to jolt the minds of his accusers into seeing Him as the fulfillment of this great prophetic passage.

As I bring this section to a close, I want to keep my promise to prove that Christ was not truly forsaken by the Father. Knowing that Psalm 22 is CLEARLY a prophecy of what would happen at Calvary, consider verse 24.

> **Psalm 22:24**
> For he hath not despised nor abhorred the affliction of the afflicted; neither hath he hid his face from him; but when he cried unto him, he heard.

I know of no Trinitarian who would ever say they believe in more than one God. Every Trinitarian with whom I have ever had this discussion claims to believe in only one – they just believe that one is made up of three separate persons.

Nevertheless, let us be honest. If the Father and Son are distinct and separate enough that one could forsake the other, there is no way they are truly "one God." If they can separate – even for a moment – then you have two Gods, plain and simple.

Questions Answered

Psalm 22:24 forever settles this issue. It is clear from this passage that at no time could it be truthfully said that God "hid his face" from the one being crucified. Thus, as you can see, the Father did NOT "turn His face away" or forsake the Son. How could He? He was dwelling IN the Son!

CHAPTER 7
CONCLUSION

As I bring this book to its completion, let me implore you to consider its contents carefully and prayerfully. The identity of God – and the Person of Jesus Christ – are doctrines which hold eternal consequences. We cannot afford to be wrong!

> **John 8:24**
> *I said therefore unto you, that ye shall die in your sins: for if ye believe not that I am he, ye shall die in your sins.*
>
> **John 8:27**
> *They understood not that he spake to them of the Father.*

I have personally witnessed literal multitudes of men and women around the globe getting a revelation of the Mighty God in Christ! Although it means rejecting many things they have believed for many years, they are seeing the beauty of this teaching and embracing it fully. As a result, many other things in the Scripture are becoming abundantly clearer to them.

It is imperative that you embrace the truth. Only the truth can provide real freedom.

Conclusion

> **John 8:32**
> *And ye shall know the truth, and the truth shall make you free.*

My friend, the Bible nowhere declares that there are "three in one." While there IS a verse that mentions "three," it does not say they are "IN" one. It says they ARE one!

> **1 John 5:7**
> *For there are three that bear record in heaven, the Father, the Word, and the Holy Ghost: and these three are one.*

Compare this with the verse immediately afterwards. It also speaks of "three," but it does not say these three ARE one.

> **1 John 5:8**
> *And there are three that bear witness in earth, the Spirit, and the water, and the blood: and these three agree in one.*

It is evident that the Spirit, the water, and the blood could never be said to actually BE one. They just "agree in one." (I provide a more in-depth explanation of this verse in my book on the New Birth.)

The Father, Word (*i.e.*, Son), and Holy Ghost, however, are not like the Spirit, water, and blood. Jesus is the Father in creation, the Son in redemption, and the Holy Ghost in regeneration. Therefore, they do not just "agree in one," THEY ARE ONE!

BIBLIOGRAPHY

BARNES, A., MURPHY, J. G., COOK, F. C., PUSEY, E. B., LEUPOLD, H. C., & FREW, R., *Barnes' Notes*. Grand Rapids, Michigan: Baker.

DAVIDSON PRESS, The Holy Bible: International Standard Version: New Testament. Yorba Linda, CA, Davidson Press.

DEVER, M., DUNCAN, J. L., MOHLER JR., R. A., MAHANEY, C. J., PIPER, J., SPROUL, R. C., MACARTHUR, J., & ANYABWILE, T. M., *Proclaiming a Cross-centered Theology*. Wheaton, IL, Crossway.

HOOKE, S. H., *The Bible in Basic English*. Cambridge, Cambridge University Press.

KRUSE, D. P., *How Is One God of One Essence Manifested in Three Persons?*, Lay Evangelism, http://www.layevangelism.com/qreference/islam/trinity.htm

SCHAFF, P., *A Popular Commentary on the New Testament*. Edinburgh, T. & T. Clark.

SLICK, M., *What is the Trinity?*, Christian Apologetics and Research Ministry, https://carm.org/what-is-the-trinity

The Common English Bible Study Bible, Nashville: The Common English Bible.

VINCENT, M. R., *Word Studies in the New Testament*. New York, Scribner.

WHITE, J., *The Nature of God.*, Alpha & Omega Ministries, http://vintage.aomin.org/natureofgod.html

ABOUT THE AUTHOR

Pastor Gregory K. Riggen was born in 1960 to (at that time) non-Christian parents, He began attending an Apostolic Pentecostal Church at the age of 11. The following year, He received the Holy Ghost and was baptized in Jesus' name. He subsequently led his entire family to the Lord. He felt a call into the ministry that summer, and preached his first message on a Wednesday night at the age of 13.

Pastor Riggen received his Th.B. from Texas Bible College in Houston. With a 4.0 average, he was valedictorian of his graduating class. He entered into full-time ministry immediately upon graduation.

At the age of 24, he accepted his first pastorate. He has pastored in Texas, Colorado, Mississippi, and Kansas.

In 1988, Pastor Riggen published his first book, "The Madness and Method of Modern Music." He has written numerous articles, as well as several lessons for Word Aflame Publications. He has also written and published two Home Bible Studies.

In 2013, Pastor Riggen was invited to Zimbabwe to address a number of Trinitarian Pentecostal pastors. That meeting resulted in more than 50 pastors and wives being baptized in Jesus' name. As a result, he founded A2Z Missions, which has since gone into the countries of Botswana, Malawi, South Africa, Swaziland, and Zambia. Literally hundreds of pastors have received the revelation of the Mighty God in Christ and have been baptized in the name of Jesus because of the teaching they received at his conferences.

Pastor Riggen has pastored the Truth Church in Olathe, Kansas for 24 years. During this time, he has been instrumental in the planting of three "daughter works.". His vision is to plant many more churches throughout the greater Kansas City metropolitan area while continuing to oversee the work in Olathe.

He and his wife, Rhonda (Yates) Riggen, have been married 40 years. They have three children and nine grandchildren.

www.ingramcontent.com/pod-product-compliance
Lightning Source LLC
Chambersburg PA
CBHW071218070526
44584CB00019B/3067